Once-a-Month Cooking

Once-a-Month Cooking

Originally published as *Dinner's Ready!*

Mimi Wilson and Mary Beth Lagerborg

St. Martin's Press
New York

This book was originally published in 1984 under the title *Dinner's Ready*.

All information in this book is presented and all recommendations are made without any guarantees on the part of the authors. The authors and publisher disclaim all liability incurred in connection with the use of this information.

Photograph of Mimi Wilson and Mary Beth Lagerborg by Clarinda Spees. Photograph of Mimi Wilson by Ken Glass.

Photographs of the Wilson and Lagerborg families copyright © 1984 by Paul Pettit. Reprinted with permission.

Library of Congress Cataloging-in-Publication Data

Wilson, Mimi.
Once-a-month cooking.

1. Cookery.   2. Menus.   3. Food-Storage.
I. Lagerborg, Mary Beth.   II. Title.
TX652.W565   1986   641.5'55   86-13836
ISBN 0-312-58478-4 (pbk.)

10 9 8 7 6 5

Contents

Acknowledgments

The following neighbors, associates, relatives, and friends have provided professional advice, recipes, child care, and encouragement—very important ingredients. We are grateful to each one of them.

Our families:
  Calvin, Kurt, Kindra, and Kevin Wilson
  Alex, Tim, Daniel, and Drew Lagerborg

Pat Agnew
Jan and Tim Altman
Barbara Anderson
Deborah Ayres
Jerilynn Blum
Diane Bogart
Jim Burghardt
Elisabeth Chubb
Charlotte Cone
Connie Cox
Chris Douglas
Irene L. Evans
Dolores Eyler
Jacci Folk
Ken and Diane Glass
Melita Hayes

Roland Hieb
Susan Keaney
Christine and Vincent
  Lagerborg
Debbie and David
  Lagerborg
Lorie Mae Leavitt
Carol Mathews (cover)
Judy McBride
Bonnie McCullough
Anne Metzler
Judy Miller
Georgiana Morrill
Kathy Pitzer
Dave Plummer
Norene Rask

Karen Seeling
Virginia Shane
Bill and Ella Spees
Clarinda Spees
Sue Stockman
Dotty Thur
Kathy Voss
Barbara West
Carol West
Dawn Wilson
Deborah Wilson
Don and Chris Wilson
Kent and Debbie
  Wilson
Tricia Woodyard

WHY I PREPARED THIS MONTH'S DINNERS LAST WEDNESDAY

A warm welcome is crucial in our home. Cal and I decided early in our marriage that when company came it wouldn't do for me to be swinging from the chandelier, or for the children to be strung from it to keep them out of my way. I consider hospitality essential toward my own family members as well. They deserve my very best if anyone does!

A warm welcome is easier when food is always on hand. The method described here of cooking a month's dinners in a day and freezing them evolved from this need. Its advantages are endless. You don't need to be having company or a baby to think of reasons you'd rather not be tied to the kitchen two or three hours each late afternoon. Perhaps you have young children, work until 5:00 P.M., want to save trips to the supermarket, or want to live within a tighter food budget.

This book is meant to be practical. Its purpose is to help you achieve a welcoming environment and stew always in the pot without you in there, too.

The method developed during a time when I knew I had to do something drastic to squeeze more time into my day. I had three young children, a busy husband, company two or three times a week, and I wanted to become involved with refugees. The Once-a-Month Cooking Method is tailor-made for anyone who is either working or busy enough to know she must be organized. I used time studies to determine where I wasted the most time and found that it was in starting from scratch with the meals each day. Now, it's not as if I had to go to the garden every day or kill the chickens. Something had to change.

I was as interested in reducing our food waste as I was in saving time. Our children, my husband, and I had seen starvation during a visit to Africa and in working with refugees. We can't box up a meal and ship it to an African child, but we do choose not to buy food and then throw it away. The money saved can be spent in so many better ways.

I began cooking one week's dinners, then two weeks', then three weeks', and now a month's dinners in one day. I found the method saves time in the kitchen and the grocery store. It saves money by squelching impulse buying and by providing something always on hand (fewer trips for fast food). It saves valuable energy—personal, appliance, and auto. It minimizes food waste. Since it depends on careful planning, the method results in greater menu variety. And it is adaptable to many family favorites; you needn't use exotic recipes.

Most of the recipes included are for casseroles because we're cooking ahead the *time-consuming* dishes. You can easily pull a roast, ham slices, steaks, or hamburgers from the freezer on days you want to serve them. A few of these appear in the sample menus.

In most cases you'll be fixing and freezing only the main course. But with that much done, you have time to be more creative with your side dishes.

A home freezer and a microwave are a great help, but not necessary. If you don't have a home freezer, though, you may be able to freeze only about three weeks' dinners and still squeeze in some ice cream, juices, and frozen vegetables.

How long will it take you to prepare all these dishes? Count on approximately five hours for the two-week cycle and eight hours for either of the one-month cycles. You may need more time or less, but you should assume (to protect your sanity) that with any of the cycles it's a full day's commitment. Chances are you'll streamline the procedure as you get used to cooking this way.

You may want to develop three or four months' menus and rotate them. It really doesn't matter, of course, whether you cook two, three, or four weeks' dinners in a day. Obviously, the degree of convenience for you is greater if you cook four, but make the method suit your needs.

The two one-month cycles and shorter two-week cycle each include grocery shopping lists, assembly instructions, and a list of the cookware and freezer containers you'll need. The two-week cycle is geared to the person who has very limited kitchen counter and freezer space, who wants to tackle the method on a smaller scale at first, or who has less time or money than is needed to cook a month's dinner entrées in a day. The two-week cycle is also ideal for small families.

The recipes in the two-week cycle, as in the one-month menus, generally serve six to eight people. If your family is smaller, you could divide each dish and package it in smaller quantities. The two-week cycle would easily last a month for a family of two or three.

Once you read about this method, it will haunt you: "Hummm . . . if I had all that in the freezer, having houseguests would be so much more fun for me. . . . I could eliminate the tension of predinner hours when the children are hungry and fussy. . . . In the summer I could be in the backyard with the family rather than over the stove. . . . I would have food for friends (or for us) in emergencies. . . . I could take dishes to the cabin on weekends and not have to cook. . . . We could remodel the kitchen without the household disintegrating. . . . I could be sane from Thanksgiving through New Year's. . . ."

I hope that the Once-a-Month Cooking method will bring as many benefits

2

and pleasures into your life as it has into mine—and into the life of my friend and co-author, Mary Beth Lagerborg. It's been a rewarding and liberating experience and we are happy to be able to share it with you in this book.

Mimi Wilson

PREPARATION BEGINS WITH A PANTRY LIST

Before you use this method, cook as you normally would this month, with a large piece of paper at your elbow. Jot down exactly what you use: how many bags of frozen peas, cans of cream of chicken soup, tea bags, how many gallons of milk. It's a tedious assignment, but the payoff comes when you are able to compile an accurate monthly shopping list. Chances are that you'll use about the same amounts of each item next month. The idea is that you will buy what you need at the store, without all the extras.

Armed with this meticulous list of what you have consumed in a month (you'll be appalled), it's time for you to compile a Pantry List. This is not a Grocery Shopping List—that comes later. A Pantry List is merely a description of what your pantry contains when it is well stocked for your needs. It contains names of items, but not quantities. A sample Pantry List is enclosed, which you should alter to fit your needs.

You don't have to have a country kitchen pantry to have a Pantry List. Tape the list on the inside of one of your cupboard doors.

I find that if I am well stocked on all of these items I can keep concocting bunches of things throughout the month. If I don't have all of this, I keep running to the store.

When you've completed your Pantry List of the staples you frequently use, take inventory. With a pencil, check any item you have run out of or are about to. Later, when you formulate your Grocery Shopping List, glance at your Pantry List and add the items you have checked. After you shop, erase the pencil marks and the Pantry List is back in operation.

Don't slip into thinking that if you don't have all this on hand you can't have company. It simply makes it easier. The *ideal* is to have your pantry so well stocked that you're always a month ahead of yourself.

What can be frozen and what can't? My motto is "If it will hold still, freeze it." You may not be quite that daring, so we've included some freezing tips in the appendix. Freezing is an excellent means of preserving natural color, flavor, and nutritive value in foods. Occasionally you'll find that the taste or texture will be altered somewhat in frozen foods, but the food will not "spoil" in the freezer. And the possibilities of these alterations can be minimized if the frozen meals are eaten within the month.

4

PANTRY LIST

Baking Supplies
Almond extract
Baking powder
Baking soda
Cornstarch
Dry cocoa
Food coloring
Marshmallows
Raisins
Semisweet chocolate
Unsweetened chocolate
Vanilla extract
Yeast

Beverages
Chocolate mix
Coffee
Decaffeinated coffee
Evaporated milk
Juices
Kool Aid®
Lemonade
Powdered buttermilk
Powdered milk
Tea

Canned
Mushrooms
Soups
  Consommé
  Cream of chicken
  Cream of mushroom
  Tomato
Tomatoes
  Paste
  Sauce
  Whole

Cereals
Bran
Cream of Wheat®
Egg Noodles
Elbow macaroni
Minute tapioca
Oatmeal
Rice
  Precooked
  Regular
Spaghetti

Condiments
Bouillon
  Beef
  Chicken
Catsup
Lemon juice
Mayonnaise
Mustard
Parmesan cheese, grated
Soy sauce
Vinegar
  Cider
  White
Wine
  Red
  Sherry
  White
Worcestershire sauce

Crackers
Graham crackers
Soda crackers

Flour
Rye

Wheat
White

Mixes
Bisquick®
Cake mixes
  Angelfood
  Chocolate
  Yellow
Gelatin
Pudding

Nuts/Snacks
Almonds
Pecans
Popcorn
Walnuts

Oils and Shortening
Corn oil
Olive oil
Vegetable shortening

Paper and Plastic Products
Aluminum foil
  Heavy-duty
  Regular
Clear wrap
Freezer bags
Freezer tape
Marker
Napkins
  Dinner
  Luncheon
Paper plates
Paper towels
Plastic utensils
Sandwich bags
Tissues
Toilet paper
Trash bags
  Kitchen
  Outdoor
Waxed paper
Wooden toothpicks

Spices and Herbs
Allspice
Basil
Bay leaves
Celery seed
Chili powder
Chives
Cinnamon
Cloves, ground
Cloves, whole
Cumin
Curry powder
Dillweed
Dry mustard
Garlic powder
Garlic salt
Ginger
Lemon pepper
Minced garlic
Minced onion
Nutmeg
Onion salt
Oregano
Paprika
Parsley
Pepper
Sage
Salt
Seasoned salt
Thyme
White pepper

Sweeteners
Corn syrup
Honey
Maple syrup
Molasses
Sugar
  Brown
  Powdered
  White

STICK TO YOUR GROCERY SHOPPING LIST

Do yourself a double favor by cleaning out your refrigerator and freezer the day you make out your shopping list. You'll make room for the food to come and form your list more accurately. Begin your Grocery List by jotting down the staples you've penciled on your Pantry List. Then spread in front of you all the recipes you would like to cook and freeze that month and your calendar. Don't try to upgrade your menus and learn the system all at once. Use one of the samples enclosed or adapt it to family recipes. You can add new recipes later.

Write on your calendar when you would like to serve which recipe, noting when you will be having company and when you will be out. Obviously, if you are all going to Grandma's for a week you will not need as much. If your husband has invited his office over for dinner you can plan to double or triple a dish. Remember to plan into your menu in-season items.

Then add to your Grocery Shopping List all the ingredients you will need for each of the recipes you'll be using. Use the table of equivalents in the Appendix if you need to convert pounds to cups or vice versa. Be sure to include a roast, hamburgers, steak, fish, or such for whenever you will be serving these. Also add any items you will need for breakfasts, lunches, snacks, and side dishes.

When you have finished listing, consolidate. How many total pounds of ground beef will you need? How many pounds of chicken? How many packages of cream cheese? I know this sounds like a lot of work, and a mountain of food, but the payoff will come when you don't have to keep running to the store. You will be tempted not to buy all this. But this is what it will take to feed your family, and they must eat! Or you'll end up back at the supermarket or eating out.

Your shopping time will be shorter if you group all similar items together: meat, dairy, produce, canned goods. If you know your supermarket well, you can do this according to aisles. You may want to use one of the sample month's menus from this book, adding to the Grocery Shopping List provided so that it meets your needs.

ATTACKING THE SUPERMARKET

Do *not* try to shop and cook in one day; it's too much work. You have to leave enough emotional energy to meet your family's needs. This is going to take a couple of hours, so make an outing of it and enjoy it. If you have children, consider trading babysitting with a friend so that each of you can have one whole morning a month for shopping. If children go with you, be sure they are well rested, fed, and pottied.

You will probably need two shopping carts, your shopping list, and a pencil to mark off the items as you buy them. A specific list is imperative if you hope to keep within a food budget. Supermarkets are set up so that in order to reach the necessities we have to walk down long aisles of other temptations. The milk, eggs, bread, and meat are either way in the back or on the far sides of the store. It's no wonder when you run to the store mid-week for "just a dozen eggs" you come home with two bags of groceries. You'll get pretzels and crackers on the way in and cereal and coffee on the way out.

On the cereal aisle the sugared cereals in their colorful boxes, with freebies promised, are placed right at children's eye level. Most of us are lazy enough not to like to reach up to the top shelf or bend down to the bottom one. And most everything we pick up we put into the cart. You will save an incredible amount of money by buying only what you *need* and then coming home and preparing it.

If you will be using ground ham, ask the butcher to grind it for you. For the ham recipes in the second sample menu, select a couple of good boneless cooked hams totaling nine to ten pounds. Ask the butcher to grind three pounds from the two ends and cut the center portion into ¾-inch dinner slices and cubes.

Buy chickens of four pounds or larger or you are paying for too much bone. If you don't see any chickens out that are that large, ask the butcher if there are some in the back.

I buy all produce at once for the month's meals. I use the most perishable items, such as grapes, bananas, and fresh vegetables at the beginning of the month and save apples, oranges, frozen vegetables, and canned fruit and vegetables for the end of the month. A milkman stocks me with milk. You may want to try buying two weeks' produce at first, then three weeks', then four until you get used to it. Or many people prefer to shop once a week for fresh produce, breads, etc. Don't be frightened by the bulging carts or your whopping bill. Believe it or not, you really did use this much food last month, and if you've shopped correctly you won't be back for a long time.

OTHER CHORES ON SHOPPING DAY

When you get home, leave the dry and canned ingredients on a counter or in sacks or a laundry basket. There's no use putting them all away and pulling them out tomorrow.

Place all the chickens that require cooking in a large pot (a canning kettle works well) or two smaller pots. Cover them with water and bring them to a boil. Turn down the heat and simmer the chickens approximately one hour, or until the meat is no longer pink inside. Turn the chickens from time to time so they don't scorch. I burned them all one time. How it hurt to throw five whole chickens in the trash! The children and I had a little ceremony.

Put your feet up and browse through a magazine while the chickens are cooking. When they're finished, pour off the broth and refrigerate it to use for chicken soup and other chicken dishes. Tomorrow before you heat the broth you will skim the fat off the top and discard it.

When the chickens have cooled, remove the meat from the bone and tear it into bite-size pieces. You can do this while the chickens are still hot if you wear rubber gloves (which you save only for cooking).

We rarely serve whole chicken pieces, because chicken stretches so much further off the bone. You can serve 10 to 12 people with one chicken in a casserole, but it would take three chickens served in pieces to feed that many people.

Before you go to bed, clear off the kitchen counters, removing any what-nots or appliances you will not be using. Put out the recipes you'll cook the next day and the containers in which you'll freeze each one. For each recipe, we've included a suggestion for the most convenient or appropriate freezer container, but you can adapt to containers you have of roughly equal size, and in many cases you could use freezer bags.

If you don't want to tie up all your 13 × 9-inch baking dishes in the freezer, you can grease them, line them with heavy aluminum foil, grease the foil, and pour in the ingredients. When the meal is frozen, you can remove it from the pan in the foil and return it to the freezer. To thaw and cook the food, slip it out of the foil and back into the pan.

Quart canning jars are handy for freezing soups or stews, but you *must* leave *at least* an inch of free space at the top of the jar because the food will expand as it freezes. Try using a piece of aluminum foil as the jar lid, screwing the band down over the foil to hold it snugly in place. This provides more room for the food to expand.

Chances are you'll have all the necessary freezer containers already on hand in your kitchen. If you don't, and you need to purchase additional items, consider the following brands:

For freezer only
Superseal®, manufactured by Eagle
Perfect Storage®, manufactured by Family Products, Incorporated
Freezette®, manufactured by Republic Molding Corporation
Hefty® Plastic Freezer Containers, manufactured by Mobil Oil Corporation
New Servin' Saver™ Food Containers, manufactured by Rubbermaid
Tupperware®, manufactured by Tupperware

For freezer and microwave or conventional oven
Heatware™, manufactured by Republic Molding Corporation
Store 'N Cook™, manufactured by Litton
Hefty® Microwave Food Container, manufactured by Mobil Oil Corporation
Tupperware® Ultra 21® Cookware
Glad-Lock™ Heavy-Duty Reclosable Freezer Bags, manufactured by Union Carbide

Seal-a-Meal®, freezer to microwave bags, manufactured by Dazey
Ziploc® Microfreez®, microwave cooking bags, manufactured by Dow Chemical Company
Rubbermaid® Heatables™ Microwave Cookware
MicroWare® Ovenware; Freeze, Heat & Serve™ Microwave Ovenware; Foodkeepers™; Warm Ups™; Oven Basics® Kitchen Classics®; and Glass MicroWare®; all manufactured by Anchor Hocking

For freezer, microwave, convection oven, and conventional oven
Professional Pyrex®, manufactured by Crown Corning
NordicWare®, manufactured by Nordic
Fire & Ice©®, manufactured by Mikasa
Rubbermaid® Microwave Cookware
Corning Ware® Cookware, manufactured by Crown Corning

Using the list on page 11, pull out your blender, food processor, mixer—any appliances and equipment you will need. Place a large empty trash can in the middle of the kitchen where it is easily in range from any direction. Rearrange and make room in your freezer if you haven't already done so.

Start Mrs. Ringle's Brisket in a crockpot if you have one. If you won't be using this recipe but have a crockpot, start a stew. The idea is that by morning you will have at least one dish completed. Then get a good night's sleep.

EQUIPMENT NEEDED FOR COOKING DAY

On cooking day you will want to reuse bowls and pans as much as possible to conserve counter and stove-top space. The following list should help you know what equipment to get out in preparation for cooking.

1 very large pot or canning kettle to cook chicken the day before cooking day (or use 2 large pots)

Food processor *or* grater, knives, and rolling pin

Blender *or* hand mixer (two-week cycle and Month #1)

Crockpot (Months #1 and #2)

Double boiler (two-week cycle)

2-quart pitcher (two-week cycle)

2 large pots, one with lid

1 large saucepan with lid

1 medium saucepan with lid

1 small saucepan

1 large skillet

1 medium skillet

1 flat baking sheet (Month #2)

1 large mixing bowl

1 medium mixing bowl

1 small mixing bowl

8 to 12 small-to-medium bowls *or* plastic bags to hold grated, sliced, or diced ingredients

Rubber gloves (for deboning chicken and mixing)

Paring knife

Colander

Wooden spoons

Wet and dry measuring cups

Measuring spoons

Kitchen scissors

Hot pads

Wire whisk

Ladle

Can opener

Rubber spatula

Metal or plastic spatula

Cutting board

Tongs

Vegetable peeler

BE GLAD IT'S COOKING DAY

Sure it will be a lot of work. But one day of work will bring great benefits in time and convenience. Even if you don't complete the whole process in one day and spill into the next, when it's done, it's done—and you'll be glad.

Cooking day is not the time to skimp on breakfast. Get dressed, eat a good breakfast, and be sure to wear supportive shoes since you'll be standing all morning. If you will have young children with you be sure they are dressed, well fed, and happily involved in an activity. Crack a window or have on a fan. Play some soothing music.

You might find it helpful to trade off child care on cooking day. Keep a friend's children one day a month while she cooks; she can keep yours on your cooking day. Better yet, cook with a friend—one day a month at her house and another at yours. The company is fun, and this arrangement leaves one person to grab ingredients, empty trash, clean off counters, and chase children.

If you do have little ones at home that day, remember that taking a few minutes here and there to see to their needs works better for all concerned than being irritable through the process.

Ready to cook? If you are using one of our sample menus, turn to the corresponding Assembly Order in this book and follow it through.

If you have room on a counter, first set out all the ingredients you will be using.

Perform All Similar Tasks at Once

Next do *all* the grating, chopping, and slicing necessary and set each ingredient aside in bowls or plastic bags: onions, cheese, nuts, carrots, celery, etc. *The secret of this method is to perform all similar tasks at once.* This step may seem tedious, but you will have accomplished a lot when it's finished.

Now assemble the dishes. If you are using the Assembly Order for Month #1, finish and freeze Mrs. Ringle's Brisket. Get the spaghetti sauce assembled and simmering. I assemble the ham dishes next because they go together so quickly. Before I know it they're in the freezer.

Place the recipes on the counter in front of you, and behind each recipe place a bowl in which to assemble it. To save time use one set of measuring cups and spoons for dry ingredients and one set for wet.

Add Common Ingredients Until They Play Out

First put into the bowls, according to each recipe, ingredients which are needed in all or most of the recipes. When the similar ingredients play out, complete one dish, then the second, then the third. Some dishes will have to be assembled individually, but still whenever possible you will do all similar processes at once: brown ground beef, sauté onions, etc.

Put each dish into its freezing container and set it aside on a table until you can take a break to wash your hands, seal the dishes, and label them. Food should be cooled to room temperature before you freeze it. Label each with its name, the date, and cooking instructions so you don't have to consult the recipe later:

AZTEC QUICHE 8/18
Bake uncovered 40–50 minutes at 325° F

If a recipe calls for grated cheese, almonds, bread crumbs, etc., to be added during baking, measure the needed ingredient and seal it in a freezer bag taped to the casserole container.

A few of the recipes, such as Veal Scallopini in Spaghetti Sauce and French Bread Pizza, are assembled from frozen ingredients on the day served.

I freeze most dishes before baking them. Part of the joy of serving good meals, after all, is the aroma from the oven as it bakes. Why deprive your family of that? That is why I also freeze balls of cookie dough instead of the baked cookies.

When you've completed the ham dishes, give the mixing bowls a quick rinse and repeat the process for the chicken dishes.

Any vegetables and chicken pieces you have left today can be thrown into the chicken soup; nothing is wasted. The chicken soup given here is great in a child's thermos, for lunch, for dinner, or to take to a sick friend.

Assemble the chicken dishes first using ingredients common to many. When the common ingredients play out, finish the first chicken dish, the second, and so on. Label and freeze them.

When you are assembling ground beef entrées, brown together all the ground beef that requires it, and sauté the onions at once. Then measure these ingredients into mixing bowls or skillets as you need them. (See the equivalency chart in the Appendix.)

Continue through your Assembly Order, taking a break of homemade chicken soup for lunch. Run the dishwasher while you're eating. Take breaks for yourself or the children when necessary. Your frame of mind is crucial, so stop when you need to. Change your shoes, sip a cold beverage, play different music; figure out what's upsetting you and deal with it.

When your dishes have all been labeled and committed to the freezer (pause to appreciate the sight!), attack your dirty kitchen and if possible go out to dinner. You've worked hard today and saved a great deal of time and money, so you can afford to treat yourself.

THE AFTERMATH

Post the month's menu you've prepared on your freezer or cupboard door to help you choose the day's dinner and to keep inventory. Check off dishes as you use them.

After dinner on any given evening, choose, select, and remove the *next* evening's dinner from the freezer and put it in the refrigerator to thaw. You may also thaw in a microwave oven or on a kitchen counter, but the food should not be left sitting out once it's thawed.

These meals really do go together in minutes of your time. Just think of all the time and energy you'll save from cooking and cleaning up. Time for your husband, your children, yourself. Time to have fun and entertain calmly. It is my hope that this method will prove as helpful to you as it has been to me.

Mimi Wilson (left) and Mary Beth Lagerborg (right)

Two-Week Cycle

Menu Calendar for
Two-Week Cycle

SUN.	MON.	TUES.	WED.	THURS.	FRI.	SAT.
		1 *Cooking Day Eat out!*	2 *Chicken Packets*	3 *Mexican Stroganoff*	4 *Sole, Crab, and Artichokes*	5 *Linguine à la Anne (Company 8)*
6 *Cheese Soup*	7 *Spaghetti*	8 *Wild Rice Chicken*	9 *Roast Beef*	10 *Marinated Flank Steak*	11 *Chicken Broccoli*	12 *Cannelloni*
13 *Baked Eggs*	14 *Pork Chops with Limas*	15 *Poulet de France*	16	17	18	19
20	21	22	23	24	25	26
27	28	29	30	31		

GROCERY SHOPPING LIST FOR TWO-WEEK CYCLE

The following is a shopping list for the two-week cooking cycle. *It assumes the staples and spices given on the Pantry List (pages 5–6) are already on hand.* An asterisk (*) after an item indicates it can be stored for use until the day its dish is served.

Canned
1 6½-ounce jar or can artichoke hearts
1 6½-ounce can crab meat or 1 4¼-ounce can shrimp or combination
1 8-ounce can sliced mushrooms
1 4-ounce can sliced mushrooms
1 4-ounce can mushroom pieces and stems
1 8-ounce can sliced water chestnuts
3 15-ounce cans tomato sauce
1 6-ounce can tomato paste
4 10¾-ounce cans cream of mushroom soup (1 can*)
2 10¾-ounce cans cream of chicken soup
1 12-ounce can evaporated milk
1 12-ounce jar chili sauce
Be sure you have on hand the 2 cups mayonnaise needed. (*)
Optional: ¼ cup green chili salsa for Mexican Stroganoff (page 28)

Dry
1 16-ounce box linguine
1 8-ounce box spaghetti*
1 box or 2 to 3 cups croutons
6 slices bread
1 package (7-pound bird size) Pepperidge Farm Seasoned Stuffing Crumbs®

1 6¼-ounce package Uncle Ben's Fast Cooking Long Grain and Wild Rice®

Frozen
1 10-ounce package frozen chopped broccoli
1 10-ounce package frozen lima beans
1 package (2 loaves) frozen Rhodes Italian Baking Dough®

Dairy
1 16-ounce package sliced mozzarella cheese
1½ pounds mild Cheddar cheese
4 ounces Romano cheese
8 eggs
1 8-ounce container sour cream*
2 packages refrigerated crescent rolls*
1 3-ounce package cream cheese
4 sticks butter or margarine (4 tablespoons*)
3 quarts milk (1 quart*)
(Be sure you have enough Parmesan cheese on hand)

Meat, Poultry, and Seafood
1 pound Italian sausage
10 pounds whole chickens *or* 8 pounds chicken breasts

2⅓ pounds cooked ham (you will need this all cubed)
2 pounds round steak (cut into bite-size pieces)
1 flank steak
8 loin pork chops
6 fillets of sole (8 to 12 ounces total weight)
Beef roast*

Produce
1 large apple
4 medium onions (½ onion*)
5 cloves garlic
1 bunch celery
2 carrots
8–10 fresh mushrooms
3 green peppers *or* 2 green peppers and 1 red pepper
Fresh parsley

SUGGESTED FREEZER CONTAINERS FOR TWO-WEEK CYCLE

The following is a list of the containers or flat baking dishes suggested for freezing each recipe in the two-week cycle. These are not, of course, the only containers in which you could freeze these foods. But they should give you an idea of the size and number of containers you'll need.

6 large freezer bags
1 small freezer bag
1 4-cup freezer container
1 6-cup freezer container

1 1½-quart baking dish
1 8-cup freezer container
4 13 × 9-inch baking dishes

ASSEMBLY ORDER FOR TWO-WEEK CYCLE

Day Before

1. Cook and debone all the chicken. Refrigerate the chicken in two freezer bags.
2. Refrigerate chicken broth. A 2-quart pitcher will hold the amount you'll need.
3. Freeze the roast.

Night Before

1. Set out the recipes, bowls, appliances, freezer containers, and canned and dry ingredients.
2. Put the frozen bread dough in the refrigerator to thaw overnight.

Begin Cooking Day

1. Brown the Italian sausage for Spaghetti Sauce in a large pot.
2. Perform all the chopping, grating, slicing necessary.
   Onions: Chop 4
   Garlic: Mince 5 cloves and keep the following in three separate mounds: 2 cloves/2 cloves/1 clove
   (Take a minute here to add the rest of the ingredients to the Italian sausage to start Spaghetti Sauce.)
   Carrots: Shred 2
   Fresh mushrooms: Slice 8 to 10
   Celery: Chop 1½ cups
   Parsley: Chop ½ cup
   Green peppers (and red pepper): Dice ¼ cup green pepper. Slice the rest of the peppers or save them whole to slice when serving the Linguine à la Anne.
   Apple: Chop 1 and sprinkle with lemon juice or wait and chop the apple when assembling pork chops.
   Cheddar cheese: Grate 24 ounces (6 cups)
   Romano cheese: Grate 8 ounces (2 cups)

Assemble Chicken Dishes

1. Cook rice for Wild Rice Chicken.
2. Start Cheese Soup.
3. In a mixing bowl assemble Chicken Packets (mixing with hands works best) and freeze.

4. In the same mixing bowl (washed and dried) now assemble Wild Rice Chicken and freeze.
5. Start Poulet de France in the mixing bowl.
6. Heat water and margarine for the stuffing in the saucepan used to cook the wild rice, after washing pan out.
7. Cook broccoli in saucepan used for stuffing.
8. Assemble and freeze Poulet de France.
9. Assemble and freeze Chicken Broccoli.
10. Cool, then freeze Cheese Soup.
11. Cool Spaghetti Sauce (don't freeze it yet).

Assemble Ham Dishes
1. Dice all the ham, placing it in two piles, 2 pounds and 1 cup.
2. Boil the linguine.
3. Assemble Baked Eggs and freeze.
4. Assemble Linguine à la Anne and freeze.

Assemble Beef Dishes
1. Assemble Cannelloni and freeze.
2. Freeze remaining Spaghetti Sauce.
3. Cut up the round steak if the butcher didn't.
4. Assemble the Mexican Stroganoff and simmer.
5. Stir the flank steak marinade ingredients in a small bowl. Put into freezer bag with the flank steak and freeze Marinated Flank Steak.

Assemble Miscellaneous Dishes
1. Begin Mornay Sauce for Sole, Crab, and Artichokes.
2. Brown the pork chops.
3. Assemble Sole, Crab, and Artichokes and freeze.
4. Cool Mexican Stroganoff.
5. Assemble Pork Chops with Limas and freeze.
6. Freeze Mexican Stroganoff.

Recipes for Two-Week Cycle

Spaghetti Sauce

1 pound Italian sausage
¾ cup finely chopped onion
1 6-ounce can tomato paste
3 15-ounce cans tomato sauce
1 cup water
2 cloves garlic, chopped

2 bay leaves
1 tablespoon sugar
2 teaspoons dried basil
1 teaspoon dried oregano
2 tablespoons chopped fresh parsley
2 teaspoons salt

Brown the sausage with the onion and drain. Add the rest of the ingredients and simmer, partly covered, for 2 hours. Simmering can be done in a crockpot, if desired. Freeze in separate containers for use in the Cannelloni (page 28) and for spaghetti.

When thawed, heat thoroughly and serve over 8 ounces cooked spaghetti.

Summary of processes:
   Chop: ¾ cup onion, 2 cloves garlic, 2 tablespoons parsley
   Freeze in: 4-cup container (for spaghetti). Note that remaining sauce
      will be packaged and frozen with Cannelloni (page 28)
   Serve with: Spaghetti, accompanied by tossed salad, fresh broccoli or
      green beans, Italian bread
Makes 4 to 6 servings

Wild Rice Chicken

1 cup cooked, deboned, diced chicken
1 8-ounce can sliced water chestnuts, drained
1 cup finely chopped celery
1¼ cups finely chopped onion
1 6¼-ounce package Uncle Ben's Fast Cooking Long Grain and Wild Rice®

1 cup mayonnaise (used on serving day)
1 10¾-ounce can cream of mushroom soup, undiluted (used on serving day)

Cook the rice according to package directions. Mix together all ingredients except the mayonnaise and soup and freeze.

When thawed, place mixture in 11 × 7-inch baking dish. Stir together the mayonnaise and the undiluted mushroom soup and spread the mixture over the top. Bake, covered, at 325° F for 1 hour.

Summary of processes

Chop: 1 cup celery, 1¼ cups onion

Freeze in: Large freezer bag

Serve with: Green beans, peach halves with cottage cheese and a maraschino cherry

Note: This is a good dish for someone recovering from surgery or an illness.

Makes 6 servings

Cheese Soup

3½ cups chicken broth
2 carrots, shredded
1 cup cooked, deboned, diced chicken
3 tablespoons sherry
1 teaspoon Worcestershire sauce
¼ teaspoon celery seed
2 cups grated mild Cheddar cheese

¾ cup chopped onion (used on serving day)
4 tablespoons butter or margarine (used on serving day)
¼ cup all-purpose flour (used on serving day)
4 cups milk (used on serving day)

In a large saucepan combine the first 6 ingredients. Bring to a boil and simmer, covered, for 1 hour. Freeze with the cheese in a freezer bag taped to the soup container.

When thawed, sauté onion in the butter. Add flour and milk to make a white sauce. Add the cheese to the white sauce to melt it. Add this sauce to the soup and heat through.

Summary of processes

Shred: 2 carrots

Grate: 2 cups mild Cheddar cheese

Freeze in: 1 8-cup freezer container

Serve with: Egg salad sandwiches, celery sticks

Makes 4 servings

Chicken Packets

2 cups cooked, deboned, diced chicken
1 3-ounce package cream cheese, at room temperature
1 tablespoon chopped chives
2 tablespoons milk
Salt to taste

2 packages refrigerated crescent rolls (used on serving day)
4 tablespoons melted butter or margarine (used on serving day)
Crushed crouton crumbs (used on serving day)

Combine the chicken, cream cheese, chives, milk, and salt. Mix very well and freeze.

When thawed, unroll 2 packages crescent rolls and press each pair into a rectangle. Place 2 heaping tablespoons of the chicken mixture into the center of each rectangle. Fold dough over and seal edges tightly. Roll each packet in melted butter and then in crouton crumbs. Place on a baking sheet and bake 20 minutes at 350 ° F.

Summary of processes
> *Chop:* 1 tablespoon chives
> *Freeze the filling in:* 1 small freezer bag
> *Serve with:* Baked apples stuffed with plump raisins

Note: These are good served either hot or cold in a lunch box.

Makes 8 packets

Poulet de France

1 package Pepperidge Farm Seasoned Stuffing Crumbs® (7-pound bird size)
1 stick margarine or butter, melted
2 cups chicken broth
3 cups cooked, deboned, diced chicken
½ cup chopped onion
¼ cup minced chives
½ cup finely chopped celery
½ cup mayonnaise
¾ teaspoon salt
2 eggs
1½ cups milk
1 10¾-ounce can cream of mushroom soup, undiluted
1 cup grated mild Cheddar cheese

Mix together the stuffing, margarine, and 1 cup broth according to package directions. Stir together the chicken, remaining 1 cup broth, onion, chives, celery, mayonnaise, and salt.

Spread half of the stuffing into the bottom of a 13 × 9-inch baking dish. Add the chicken mixture. Top with the remaining stuffing. Whisk together the eggs, milk, and soup and pour evenly over the top. Freeze with the cheese in a bag attached. When thawed, bake, covered, for 40 minutes at 325° F. After 30 minutes, sprinkle with cheese and continue to bake, uncovered, for the last 10 minutes.

Summary of processes

Chop: ½ cup onions, ½ cup celery
Mince: ¼ cup chives
Grate: 1 cup mild Cheddar cheese
Freeze in: 13 × 9-inch baking dish
Serve with: Lemon gelatin salad, frozen peas. This is a super dish to take to a pot luck. Garnish with half slices of red spiced apples.

Makes 8 servings

Chicken Broccoli

1 10-ounce package frozen chopped broccoli
4 cups cooked, deboned, diced chicken
2 10¾-ounce cans cream of chicken soup, undiluted
½ cup mayonnaise
1 4-ounce can sliced mushrooms
¼ teaspoon curry powder (more if you like curry)
3 tablespoons sherry
¾ cup grated Parmesan cheese

Cook the broccoli slightly in boiling water and spread it on the bottom of a greased 13 × 9-inch baking dish. Stir together the chicken, soup, mayonnaise, mushrooms, curry powder, sherry, and ½ cup of the Parmesan cheese and spread on top of the broccoli. Top with the remaining ¼ cup Parmesan cheese. Freeze.

When thawed, bake, covered, at 350° F for 40 minutes. Uncover and bake another 20 minutes.

Summary of processes

Freeze in: 13 × 9-inch greased baking dish
Serve with: Homemade bread, Cranberry Cream Salad (page 97)
Makes 6 to 8 servings

Baked Eggs

6 bread slices, cut into cubes
3 cups grated mild Cheddar cheese
1 cup cooked cubed ham
¼ cup chopped green pepper
½ cup chopped onion
6 eggs
3 cups milk

Combine all ingredients except the eggs and milk in a 13 × 9-inch baking dish. Whisk together the eggs and milk and pour over the top. Refrigerate overnight to serve tomorrow morning, or freeze the dish.

When thawed, bake, uncovered, at 375° F for 45 minutes.

Summary of processes
    Grate: 3 cups mild Cheddar cheese
    Chop: ¼ cup green pepper, ½ cup onion
    Freeze in: 13 × 9-inch baking dish
    Serve with: Sweet roll, grapefruit or orange slices

Note: This is also good substituting 6 slices cooked crumbled bacon for the ham.

Makes 8 to 10 servings

Linguine à la Anne

1 pound linguine
6 cups (2 pounds) cooked cubed ham
1 stick butter or margarine (½ stick used on preparation day, ½ stick used on serving day)
1 4-ounce can mushroom stems and pieces
¼ cup all-purpose flour

1 teaspoon salt
1⅓ cups water
1 12-ounce can evaporated milk
1 chicken bouillon cube
½ cup grated Romano cheese
1 each red and green pepper, sliced (used on serving day)
1 cup croutons (used on serving day)

Cook the linguine according to package directions and drain. Return it to the pot you boiled it in.

Melt 4 tablespoons of the butter in a saucepan. Blend in the flour and salt, then the liquid drained from the mushrooms, the water, evaporated milk, and bouillon cube. Bring to a boil and stir the sauce a minute or two until it thickens.

Add 2 cups of the sauce and the drained mushrooms to the linguine and toss until well mixed. Spoon the linguine mixture into a 13 × 9-inch baking dish, pressing it up the sides to leave a slight hollow in the center of the dish.

Toss the ham in the remaining sauce and spoon it into the hollow in the pasta. Sprinkle with Romano cheese and freeze.

When thawed, bake the casserole, uncovered, for 20 minutes at 400 ° F. Meanwhile sauté the sliced peppers in the remaining butter until soft. When serving, sprinkle croutons around the edge of the casserole and mound the center with sautéed red and green peppers.

Summary of processes
    Slice: 1 red pepper and 1 green pepper
    Freeze in: 13 × 9-inch baking dish
    Serve with: Spinach salad, beets, croissants
Makes 8 servings

Cannelloni

1 16-ounce package sliced mozzarella   Spaghetti Sauce (see page 23)
   cheese
1 package (2 loaves) frozen Rhodes
   Italian Baking Dough®

Thaw the two loaves of dough. Divide each loaf into 5 parts and pull each part into a square. Ladle ⅓ to ½ cup spaghetti sauce onto the center of each square. Place a half slice of mozzarella, folded to fit, on top of the sauce.

Fold the dough over to form a turnover and pinch edges to seal. Place another half cheese slice on top of each turnover and wrap each packet in a sandwich bag. Freeze in freezer bags with 5 turnovers per bag, including some extra sauce in a sealed bag.

These turnovers are easier to handle if baked while still frozen. Remove the cheese slices from the tops of the turnovers. Place the turnovers on a greased baking sheet and bake at 350° F for about 20 minutes, until golden brown. Add the cheese slices to the top during the last 5 minutes of baking. Serve with extra warmed sauce ladled on top.

Summary of processes
    Freeze in: 3 large freezer bags
    Serve with: Tossed salad with Italian dressing and Fresh Baked Asparagus (page 97) or broccoli
Makes 10 servings

Mexican Stroganoff

2 pounds round steak, cut in bite-size   2 teaspoons seasoned salt
   pieces   1 teaspoon soy sauce
1 cup finely chopped onion   1 8-ounce can sliced mushrooms,
2 cloves garlic, minced   drained
2 tablespoons cooking oil   (Optional: you can add ¼ cup green
2 cups water (or 1 cup red wine and   chili salsa for extra zip)
   ½ cup water)   1 8-ounce container sour cream (used
½ cup chili sauce   on serving day)
1 tablespoon paprika   3 tablespoons flour (used on serving
1 tablespoon chili powder   day)

Brown the meat, onion, and garlic in oil in a large saucepan. Drain. Add next 7 ingredients to the meat and simmer, covered, 1 hour or until meat is tender. Freeze.

When thawed, warm the meat mixture. Stir together the sour cream and flour and add to the meat 5 to 10 minutes before serving. Serve over noodles or rice.

Summary of processes
    Cut up: Round steak
    Chop: 1 cup onion
    Mince: 2 cloves garlic
    Freeze in: 6-cup freezer container
    Serve with: Rice or noodles, tomatoes stuffed with guacamole, warm tortillas, corn on the cob
Makes 6 to 8 servings

Marinated Flank Steak

½ cup vegetable oil
¼ cup soy sauce
¼ cup sherry
2 teaspoons Worcestershire sauce

½ teaspoon ginger
1 minced clove garlic
1 flank steak

Combine all ingredients except the flank steak. Pour over the flank steak in a freezer bag and freeze with the flank steak in the marinade.

When thawed, remove the flank steak from the marinade and barbecue or broil it 8 to 12 minutes per side. Slice it against the grain thinly, cutting diagonally.

Summary of processes
    Mince: 1 clove garlic
    Freeze in: Large freezer bag
    Serve with: Twice-Baked Potatoes Deluxe (page 95), peas, Frozen Fruit Medley (page 97)
Makes 4 servings

Sole, Crab, and Artichokes

Mornay Sauce
¼ cup soft butter or margarine
1 teaspoon salt
¼ cup flour
¼ teaspoon white pepper

2 cups hot milk
¼ cup grated Romano cheese
¼ cup grated Parmesan cheese

8 to 10 fresh mushrooms
1 to 2 tablespoons butter or
  margarine
6 fillets of sole (about 8 to 12 ounces)
1 6½-ounce can crab, or 1 4¼-ounce

can shrimp, or a combination of
  both
Chopped fresh parsley
1 6½-ounce can or jar artichoke
  hearts

Pour all Mornay Sauce ingredients in a blender. Cover and blend on high for 30 seconds. Pour in top of a double boiler and cook over simmering water for 15 minutes, stirring occasionally *or* thicken in a microwave oven.

Meanwhile lightly sauté the mushrooms in 1 to 2 tablespoons butter. Roll the sole fillets around the crab, shrimp, or combination. Place rolls in a greased 1½-quart baking dish. Cover with the Mornay Sauce. Sprinkle with chopped parsley and arrange the mushrooms and artichokes around the rim of the dish. Freeze.

When thawed, bake, uncovered, for 30 minutes at 350° F.

Summary of processes
> *Slice:* 8 to 10 fresh mushrooms
> *Freeze in:* 1½-quart baking dish
> *Serve with:* Lemon Rice (page 94), peas, blueberry muffins

Makes 4 to 6 servings

Pork Chops and Limas

8 loin pork chops
1 10-ounce package frozen lima beans
1 large apple, chopped

2 10¾-ounce cans cream of
  mushroom soup, undiluted
1 teaspoon dried sage
Salt and pepper to taste

Brown pork chops in large skillet. Drain and cool on paper towel. Meanwhile run cold water over the lima beans to separate them (do not thaw them). Mix together all ingredients except the pork chops and place in freezer bag. Add chops to the freezer bag and freeze.

When thawed, bake, covered, at 350 ° F for 1 hour.

Summary of processes
> *Chop:* 1 large apple
> *Freeze in:* Large freezer bag
> *Serve with:* Mashed potatoes (don't waste that good gravy) and spicy
>   apple sauce

Makes 4 to 8 servings, depending on size of pork chops

Mimi Wilson

Month #1

Menu Calendar for
Month #1

SUN.	MON.	TUES.	WED.	THURS.	FRI.	SAT.
				1 *Cooking Day Eat out!*	2 *Manicotti*	3 *Poulet de France (Company 8)*
4 *Baked Eggs*	5 *Steak*	6 *Ham & Swiss Pastry Bake*	7 *Cheesy Corn Casserole*	8 *Veal Scallopini in Spaghetti Sauce*	9 *Hamburgers*	10 *Mimi's Chicken Soup*
11 *Eat Out*	12 *Ham Loaf*	13 *Barbecued Fillets*	14 *Pork Chops on Rice*	15 *Shrimp Creole Luncheon 6*	16 *Spaghetti*	17 *Out Children & Sitter Chicken Packets*
18 *Aztec Quiche*	19 *Wild Rice Chicken*	20 *Taco Pie*	21 *Linguine à la Anne*	22 *Eat Out*	23 *French Bread Pizza*	24 *Ham Slices*
25 *Ravioli Soup*	26 *Heavenly Chicken (Company 8)*	27 *Eat Out*	28 *Brisket*	29 *Ham Loaf*	30 *Joes to Go*	31 *Fruity Curried Chicken*

35

GROCERY SHOPPING LIST FOR MONTH #1

The following is a shopping list for the recipes in sample month #1. *It assumes the staples and spices given on the Pantry List are already on hand.* An asterisk (*) after an item indicates it can be stored for use until the day its dish is served.

Canned

1 8-ounce jar chili sauce
1 2-ounce can mushroom stems and pieces
1 4-ounce can mushroom stems and pieces
6 15-ounce cans tomato sauce
3 8-ounce cans tomato sauce
1 28-ounce can tomato sauce
1 6-ounce can tomato paste
1 12-ounce can tomato paste
2 4-ounce cans diced green chilies
1 8-ounce can sliced water chestnuts
1 17-ounce can whole kernel corn
1 10¾-ounce can cream of chicken soup
2 10¾-ounce cans cream of mushroom soup (1 can*)
1 14½-ounce can beef broth
1 8¾-ounce can apricots
1 12-ounce can evaporated milk
Be sure you have on hand at least 2 cups mayonnaise
Optional: 10-ounce jar apricot jam for Ham Loaf* (page 44)

Dry

1 16-ounce box linguine
1 8-ounce box spaghetti
1 box small pasta or soup macaroni (1 cup needed)

1 8-ounce box manicotti
Italian flavored bread crumbs*
1 6½-ounce box Uncle Ben's Fast Cooking Long Grain and Wild Rice®
1 package (7-pound bird size) Pepperidge Farm Seasoned Stuffing Crumbs®
1 package onion soup mix
1 envelope taco seasoning mix
Whole cloves
4 ounces slivered almonds*
4 ounces raisins
1 loaf French bread*
12 hamburger buns plus enough for serving hamburgers
7 slices bread
Croutons* (at least 2 to 3 cups needed)
Be sure you have on hand 2 cups raw rice (1 cup*) and crackers for 3 cups cracker crumbs

Frozen

1 10-ounce package frozen chopped spinach
1 10-ounce package frozen peas*
1 small can frozen orange juice
1 12-ounce package frozen ravioli (plain, without sauce)*

2 9-inch deep-dish frozen pie shells
(1*)
1½ cups frozen salad shrimp, peeled
and deveined*

Dairy
3¼ sticks butter or margarine
(1 stick*)
2 packages refrigerated crescent
rolls*
1 12-ounce container cottage cheese
with chives
1 16-ounce container cottage cheese
1 15-ounce container ricotta cheese
2½ quarts milk (or use powdered
milk)
1 cup half and half
2 dozen eggs (1 dozen*)
1½ pounds mozzarella cheese
4 ounces Swiss cheese
2 pounds mild Cheddar cheese
1 8-ounce package Monterey Jack
cheese
1 3-ounce package cream cheese
Grated Parmesan cheese (at least 4
cups)
2 ounces grated Romano cheese
Optional: Sour cream for Taco Pie
(page 53)*

Meat, Poultry, and Seafood
12 ounces bacon
1 pound Italian sausage

Steaks—enough for the family*
1 large beef brisket
9 pounds lean ground beef *plus*
enough to feed your family
hamburgers*
1 pound very thin boneless veal
cutlets*
9 to 10 pounds boneless cooked ham
with 4 pounds of it cubed, 3 pounds
ground (from the two ends), and
the center portion cut in dinner
slices*
6 ¾-inch-thick pork chops
9 pounds whole chickens *or* 7 pounds
breasts only *plus* 8 large chicken
breast halves
Optional: Pastrami slices for French
Bread Pizza (page 42)*

Produce
1 whole head garlic (1 clove*)
9 medium onions
1 bunch green onions
3 large green peppers (two*) *or* 2
large green peppers (one*) and 1
red pepper*
1 bunch celery
3 carrots
Fresh parsley
Optional: Lettuce and tomato for
Taco Pie (page 53)*
Optional: ⅓ fresh pineapple for Ham
Loaf (page 44)*

SUGGESTED FREEZER CONTAINERS FOR MONTH #1

Heavy aluminum foil (for French Bread)
1 small freezer bag
10 large freezer bags
2 2-cup freezer containers
2 6-cup freezer containers
2 8-cup freezer containers
1 16-cup freezer container

2 loaf pans (or use 2 large freezer bags)
1 9-inch quiche or pie pan
1 10-inch quiche or pie pan
1 11 × 7-inch baking dish
1 3-quart casserole of any shape
4 13 × 9-inch baking dishes

ASSEMBLY ORDER FOR MONTH #1

Day Before
1. Cook and debone all the chicken *except* 8 breast halves. Cover the chickens with at least 6 quarts of water so you'll have enough broth to make Mimi's Chicken Soup tomorrow. Wear rubber gloves if you debone the chicken while it's hot.
2. Refrigerate the chicken and the chicken broth.
3. In freezer bags, freeze the veal cutlets, steaks, ham dinner slices, ground beef for hamburgers, hamburger buns, and French bread. You will not need to use any of these until the days you serve them.

Night Before
1. Set out recipes, bowls, appliances, freezing containers, and canned and dry ingredients.
2. Start Mrs. Ringle's Brisket in a crockpot.

Begin Cooking Day
1. Cool, slice, and freeze the brisket in its broth. Wash out the crockpot.
2. Mix 10 cups milk from milk powder (optional).
3. Grease casserole dishes that will require it.
4. Skim fat from chicken broth and discard the fat.
5. Perform all chopping, grating, slicing, and crushing necessary.
   Ham: Dice 9 cups if your butcher didn't do this.
   Onions: Chop 7, leaving the 8th onion whole for Mimi's Chicken Soup.
     Open windows and keep tissues handy.
   Green onions: Chop 1 cup
   Green peppers: Chop 1, slice 1*
   Red pepper: Slice 1*
   Celery: Slice 2¼ cups
   Carrots: Shred 3
   Garlic: Mince 6 cloves
   Parsley: Chop ¾ cup
   Mozzarella cheese: Slice 12 ounces, grate 8 ounces
   Monterey Jack cheese: Grate 8 ounces
   Mild Cheddar cheese: Grate 8 cups
   Cracker crumbs: Crush 3 cups
6. Start Spaghetti Sauce in crockpot.

Assemble Ham Dishes

1. Boil the linguine for Linguine à la Anne (set timer) while you assemble Ham Loaf.
2. Assemble Linguine à la Anne.
3. Assemble Ham and Swiss Pastry Bake.
4. Freeze ham dishes.

Assemble Chicken Dishes

1. Prepare in separate saucepans the rice for Wild Rice Chicken and that for Fruity Curried Chicken.
2. Meanwhile in 3 bowls assemble the remaining ingredients for Chicken Packets, Wild Rice Chicken, and Fruity Curried Chicken.
3. Add rice and freeze the dishes.
4. Begin to cook the spinach and make the white sauce for Heavenly Chicken. Assemble Heavenly Chicken.
5. Assemble Poulet de France. Freeze.
6. With the remaining chicken broth make Mimi's Chicken Soup and let simmer.

Assemble Miscellaneous Dishes

1. Assemble Pork Chops on Rice.
2. Assemble Shrimp Creole.
3. Assemble Aztec Quiche and Baked Eggs. If you use bacon for the Baked Eggs, while you are frying it fry 5 slices till limp for the Barbecued Fillets.
4. Freeze miscellaneous dishes and cool the Spaghetti Sauce.

Assemble Beef Dishes

1. Boil the manicotti. Meanwhile assemble the Barbecued Fillets.
2. Brown the ground beef for Ravioli Soup, Taco Pie, Joes to Go, and Cheesy Corn Casserole together in a large skillet. Sauté the onions for the first two dishes in a small skillet.
3. Assemble Ravioli Soup and let it simmer while you assemble the remaining recipes.
4. Assemble Manicotti and freeze the remaining Spaghetti Sauce.
5. Assemble the Taco Pie, Joes to Go, and Cheesy Corn Casserole.
6. Freeze the beef dishes. Freeze the two simmering soups after they've cooled.

You made it! Hooray!!!

Recipes for Month #1

Mrs. Ringle's Brisket

1 large brisket (4 to 6 pounds)   1 package onion soup mix
Mustard

Place the brisket, fat side up, in a crockpot. Do not add any water or liquid. Cover with mustard and the onion soup mix. Cook on low overnight.

Skim the seasonings off into the juice. Peel off and discard the fat. Slice or shred the meat and freeze in the gravy (thicken the gravy if desired).

When thawed, heat the slices in the gravy. These may be served as is or as hot roast beef sandwiches.

Summary of processes
Freeze in: 2 large freezer bags
Serve with: Twice-Baked Potatoes Deluxe (page 95)
Makes 8 to 10 servings

Veal Scallopini in Spaghetti Sauce

(Or try this with boneless chicken breast. This recipe is assembled on the day served.)

1 pound very thin veal cutlets (or   3 tablespoons vegetable or olive oil
   boneless chicken breasts)   1 clove garlic, sliced
2 cups Spaghetti Sauce (page 42)   4 slices mozzarella or Muenster
1 egg   cheese
Italian-flavored bread crumbs   Grated Parmesan cheese

Thaw the veal cutlets and one 2-cup freezer container of Spaghetti Sauce. Beat the egg with fork to combine. Sprinkle the Italian-flavored bread crumbs on a sheet of waxed paper. Dip veal into egg, then crumbs, turning it until it is coated completely.

In a large skillet heat the oil with the garlic over medium or medium-high heat. Add veal and sauté 4 minutes on each side, until golden brown.

Top each piece of veal with a cheese slice. Pour the Spaghetti Sauce around the veal. Simmer, covered, 5 minutes or until cheese is melted. Sprinkle Parmesan cheese on top.

Summary of processes
> *Slice:* 1 clove garlic, 4 slices mozzarella or Muenster cheese
> *Freeze in:* Freeze veal and the plastic-wrapped cheese slices in a large freezer bag
> *Serve with:* Spinach noodles, Italian bread, tossed salad

Makes 4 servings

French Bread Pizza

This recipe is assembled on the day served.

1 loaf French bread
2 cups Spaghetti Sauce (below)
Grated Parmesan cheese

Pastrami slices (optional)
12 ounces mozzarella cheese, sliced

On serving day, thaw the French bread, a 2-cup container of Spaghetti Sauce, and the pastrami and cheese slices. Slice the loaf of French bread in half lengthwise. On each half layer Spaghetti Sauce, Parmesan cheese, pastrami, mozzarella cheese. Broil on a baking sheet until the mozzarella is melted and cut into serving-sized pieces.

Summary of processes
> *Slice:* 12 ounces mozzarella cheese
> *Freeze in:* Freeze plastic-wrapped pastrami and mozzarella slices in separate freezer bags. Freeze French bread in heavy foil
> *Serve with:* Tossed salad, apple and orange slices

Makes 6 to 8 servings

Spaghetti Sauce

For spaghetti, Manicotti (page 52), French Bread Pizza (above), and Veal Scallopini in Spaghetti Sauce (page 41).

1 pound Italian sausage
1½ cups finely chopped onion
1 12-ounce can tomato paste
5 15-ounce cans tomato sauce
1 cup water
4 cloves garlic, chopped

4 bay leaves
2 tablespoons sugar
4 teaspoons basil
2 teaspoons oregano
4 tablespoons parsley
4 teaspoons salt

Brown the sausage with the onion and drain. Add the rest of the ingredients and bring to a boil. Reduce heat and simmer, uncovered, for 2 hours. Simmering can be done in a crockpot if desired. Freeze in separate containers for use with spaghetti (4 cups), Veal Scallopini in Spaghetti Sauce (3 cups), and French Bread Pizza (3 cups). Leave out approximately 2 cups for use in Manicotti (page 52).

When thawed, heat thoroughly the 2 cups Spaghetti Sauce and serve over 8 ounces cooked spaghetti.

Summary of processes

Chop: 1½ cups onion, 4 cloves garlic, 4 tablespoons parsley

Freeze in: 1 6-cup container and 2 2-cup containers, with about 2 cups left out for use in the Manicotti

Serve with: Tossed salad, fresh broccoli or green beans, Italian bread

Makes 4 to 6 servings over spaghetti

Linguine à la Anne

1 pound linguine
6 cups (2 pounds) cooked cubed ham
1 stick butter or margarine (½ stick used on preparation day, ½ stick used on serving day)
1 4-ounce can mushroom stems and pieces
¼ cup all-purpose flour

1 teaspoon salt
1⅓ cups water
1 12-ounce can evaporated milk
1 chicken bouillon cube
½ cup grated Romano cheese
1 each red and green pepper, sliced (used on serving day)
1 cup croutons (used on serving day)

Cook the linguine according to package directions and drain. Return it to the pot you boiled it in.

Melt 4 tablespoons of the butter in a saucepan. Blend in the flour and salt, then the liquid drained from the mushrooms, the water, evaporated milk, and bouillon cube. Bring to a boil and stir the sauce a minute or two until it thickens.

Add 2 cups of the sauce and the drained mushrooms to the linguine and toss until well mixed. Spoon the linguine mixture into a 13 × 9-inch baking dish, pressing it up the sides to leave a slight hollow in the center of the dish.

Toss the ham in the remaining sauce and spoon it into the hollow in the pasta. Sprinkle with Romano cheese and freeze.

When thawed, bake the casserole for 20 minutes, uncovered, at 400 ° F. Meanwhile sauté the sliced peppers in the remaining butter until soft. When serving sprinkle croutons around the edge of the casserole and mound the center with sautéed red and green peppers.

Summary of processes
Summary of processes
Slice: 1 red pepper and 1 green pepper
Freeze in: 1 13 × 9-inch baking dish
Serve with: Spinach salad, beets, croissants
Makes 8 servings

Ham Loaf

7½ cups (3 pounds) ground cooked ham
1½ pounds lean ground beef
3 eggs
1½ tablespoons mustard
1 teaspoon salt
2¼ cups milk

1½ cups cracker crumbs (crush in blender with crumbs needed for other recipes)
Optional: ⅓ fresh pineapple (used on serving day)
Optional: 1 small jar apricot jam (used on serving day)

Combine all ingredients. Divide into 2 loaf pans and freeze.

When thawed, bake, covered, at 325° F for 1 hour. During the last 45 minutes of baking, if desired, make slits in the loaf and stick in whole fresh pineapple slices. Serve hot or cold, dressed up with apricot jam spread over the loaf (if you didn't use the pineapple slices) or with the following sauce.

Ham Sauce (used on serving day)

¾ cup brown sugar
2 to 3 teaspoons mustard
2 teaspoons water

2 to 3 teaspoons vinegar or lemon juice

Stir together all ingredients and pour over loaf.

Summary of processes
Crush: 1½ cups cracker crumbs
Freeze in: 2 loaf pans
Serve with: Hot Spiced Fruit (page 98) and baked potatoes
Each loaf makes 6 servings

Ham and Swiss Pastry Bake

2 cups cooked cubed ham
1 cup grated Swiss cheese
¼ cup finely chopped celery
¼ cup finely chopped green pepper
2 tablespoons minced onion
1 teaspoon dry mustard

1 tablespoon lemon juice
⅓ cup mayonnaise or salad dressing (used on serving day)
1 9-inch deep-dish frozen pie shell (used on serving day)

Combine the first 7 ingredients and package in a freezer bag. Freeze.

When thawed, add the mayonnaise and pour into the 9-inch pie shell. Bake, uncovered, 25 to 35 minutes at 375° F until golden brown. Serve hot.

Summary of processes

> *Grate:* 1 cup Swiss cheese
> *Chop:* ¼ cup celery, ¼ cup green pepper
> *Freeze in:* Freeze filling in a large freezer bag
> *Serve with:* Mimi's Chicken Soup (page 48), tossed green salad

Makes 6 servings

Chicken Packets

2 cups cooked, deboned, diced chicken
1 3-ounce package cream cheese, softened
1 tablespoon chopped chives
2 tablespoons milk
Salt to taste

2 packages refrigerated crescent rolls (used on serving day)
4 tablespoons melted butter or margarine (use on serving day)
Crushed crouton crumbs (used on serving day)

Combine the chicken, cream cheese, chives, milk, and salt. Mix very well and freeze in freezer bags.

When thawed, unroll 2 packages crescent rolls and press each pair into a rectangle. Place 2 heaping tablespoons of the chicken mixture into the center of each rectangle. Fold dough over and seal edges tightly. Roll each packet in melted butter and then in crouton crumbs. Place on a baking sheet and bake 20 minutes at 350° F.

Summary of processes

> *Chop:* 1 tablespoon chives
> *Freeze in:* Freeze filling in a small freezer bag
> *Serve with:* Baked apples stuffed with plump raisins

Note: These are good served either hot or cold in a lunch box.

Makes 8 packets

Wild Rice Chicken

1 cup cooked, deboned, diced chicken
1 8-ounce can sliced water chestnuts, drained
1 cup finely chopped celery
1¼ cups finely chopped onion
1 6¼-ounce package Uncle Ben's Fast Cooking Long Grain and Wild Rice®

1 cup mayonnaise (used on serving day)
1 10¾-ounce can cream of mushroom soup, undiluted (used on serving day)

Cook the rice according to package directions. Mix together all ingredients except the mayonnaise and soup and freeze.

When thawed, place mixture in 11 × 7-inch baking dish. Stir together the mayonnaise and the undiluted mushroom soup and spread the mixture over the top. Bake, covered, at 325° F for 1 hour.

Summary of processes
Chop: 1 cup celery, 1¼ cups onion
Freeze in: Large freezer bag
Serve with: Green beans, peach halves with cottage cheese and a maraschino cherry

Note: This is a good dish for someone recovering from surgery or an illness.

Makes 6 servings

Fruity Curried Chicken

1 cup raw rice
1½ cups chopped onion
2½ cups chicken broth
3 cups cooked, deboned, diced chicken
1 teaspoon salt

½ teaspoon curry powder
¼ teaspoon pepper
1 tablespoon lemon juice
1 8¾-ounce can apricots, drained
½ cup raisins

Boil the rice and onion in the 2½ cups chicken broth, covered, for 15 minutes. Add remaining ingredients and freeze.

When thawed, bake, covered, at 350° F for 1 hour.

Summary of processes
Chop: 1½ cups onion
Freeze in: 6-cup freezer container
Serve with: Orange gelatin salad, Fresh Baked Asparagus (page 97)
Makes 6 servings

Heavenly Chicken

½ cup sliced green onion
2 tablespoons butter or margarine
2 tablespoons flour
1 cup milk
1½ cups cracker crumbs
1½ cups grated Parmesan cheese
8 large chicken breast halves,
   skinned

1 10-ounce package frozen chopped
   spinach, cooked according to
   package directions and well
   drained
1 cup cooked cubed ham

In a saucepan sauté the onion in butter until tender. Blend in flour; stir in milk all at once. Bring to a boil and cook and stir until the sauce is thickened and bubbly.

Meanwhile, combine the cracker crumbs and cheese. Dip chicken breast halves in the crumb mixture to coat lightly. Arrange the breast halves in a greased 13 × 9-inch baking dish. Seal the remaining crumb mixture in a freezer bag.

Stir the spinach and ham into the white sauce. Spoon the spinach mixture over the chicken. Freeze with the crumb mixture bag taped to the side.

When thawed, bake, covered, at 350° F for 60 to 75 minutes. Uncover and sprinkle with crumbs. Bake 10 minutes more.

Summary of processes

Crush: 1½ cup cracker crumbs
Slice: ½ cup green onion
Freeze in: 13 × 9-inch baking dish
Serve with: Zucchini, peas and carrots cooked with a little onion, pineapple and mandarin orange salad with coconut sprinkled on top

Makes 8 servings

Poulet de France

1 package Pepperidge Farm Seasoned
   Stuffing Crumbs® (7-pound bird
   size)
1 stick margarine or butter, melted
2 cups chicken broth
3 cups cooked, deboned, diced chicken
½ cup chopped onion
¼ cup minced chives

½ cup finely chopped celery
½ cup mayonnaise
¾ teaspoon salt
2 eggs
1½ cups milk
1 10¾-ounce can cream of mushroom
   soup
1 cup grated mild Cheddar cheese

Mix together the stuffing, margarine, and 1 cup broth according to package directions. Stir together the chicken, remaining 1 cup broth, onion, chives, celery, mayonnaise, and salt.

Spread half of the stuffing into the bottom of a 13 × 9-inch baking dish. Add the chicken mixture. Top with the remaining stuffing. Whisk together the eggs, milk, and soup and pour evenly over the top. Freeze with the cheese in a bag attached. When thawed, bake, covered, for 40 minutes at 325° F. After 30 minutes, sprinkle with cheese and continue to bake, uncovered, for the last 10 minutes.

Summary of processes

Chop: ½ cup onions, ½ cup celery
Mince: ¼ cup chives
Grate: 1 cup mild Cheddar cheese
Freeze in: 13 × 9-inch baking dish
Serve with: Lemon gelatin salad, frozen peas. This is a super dish to take to a pot luck. Garnish with half slices of red spiced apples

Makes 8 servings

Mimi's Chicken Soup

4 quarts chicken broth
1 small onion (peeled, ends cut off) studded with 4 or 5 whole cloves
3 carrots, shredded
½ cup sliced celery with leaves

1 cup small pasta or soup macaroni
1 tablespoon chopped fresh parsley
1 tablespoon salt
1 cup cooked, deboned, diced chicken

Combine all ingredients in a large pot. Bring to a boil and simmer, uncovered, 2 hours. Freeze.

When thawed, heat thoroughly and serve.

Summary of processes

Shred: 3 carrots
Slice: ½ cup celery
Chop: 1 tablespoon parsley
Freeze in: 1 16-cup freezer container
Serve with: Toasted cheese sandwiches and sweet pickles
Makes 12 to 15 servings

Pork Chops on Rice

6 ¾-inch thick pork chops
Salt and pepper
1 cup orange juice

1 10¾-ounce can cream of chicken
  soup
1 cup raw rice (used on serving day)

Brown the pork chops in a heavy skillet and season with salt and pepper. Mix the orange juice with the chicken soup. Seal in a freezer bag with the pork chops and freeze.

After thawing, sprinkle the rice in a greased 12 × 7½-inch baking dish. Pour half of the orange juice mixture over the rice. Arrange the pork chops on top of the rice and cover with the remaining liquid. Cover and bake at 350° F for 45 minutes. Uncover, turn off the oven, and leave in the oven 10 minutes longer.

Summary of processes
> *Freeze in:* Large freezer bag
> *Serve with:* Broccoli, cinnamon applesauce

Makes 6 servings

Shrimp Creole

⅓ cup chopped green pepper
¼ cup chopped green onion
¼ cup butter or margarine
¼ cup flour
½ teaspoon salt
Dash pepper
1 15-ounce can tomato sauce

1½ cups frozen salad shrimp, peeled
  and deveined (used on serving day)
1 10-ounce box frozen peas (used on
  serving day)
1½ cups grated mild Cheddar cheese
  (used on serving day)

Sauté the green pepper and green onion in the butter. Stir in the flour, salt, pepper, and tomato sauce. Bring this sauce to a boil and stir until it thickens.

Freeze this sauce in a freezer bag. Leave the shrimp and peas frozen and freeze the cheese in a bag attached to the sauce bag.

When thawed, combine all ingredients and bake uncovered at 450° F for 20 minutes.

Summary of processes
> *Chop:* ⅓ cup green pepper, ¼ cup green onion
> *Grate:* 1½ cups mild Cheddar cheese
> *Freeze in:* Large freezer bag
> *Serve with:* Green Rice (page 94), muffins

Note: If you have any leftover Shrimp Creole, serve it over a cheese omelet!

Makes 6 servings

Aztec Quiche

1½ cups grated Monterey Jack
    cheese
1 cup grated mild Cheddar cheese
1 9-inch deep-dish frozen pie shell
1 4-ounce can diced green chilies

1 cup half and half
3 eggs, beaten lightly
½ teaspoon salt
⅛ teaspoon cumin

Spread Monterey Jack cheese and half of the Cheddar over the bottom of the pie shell. Sprinkle diced chilies over the cheeses. Combine the half and half, eggs, and seasonings. Pour carefully into pie shell. Top with remaining Cheddar. Freeze.

When thawed, bake, uncovered, at 325° F for 40 to 50 minutes.

Summary of processes
    Grate: 1½ cups Monterey Jack cheese, 1 cup mild Cheddar cheese
    Freeze in: 9-inch oven-proof quiche or pie pan. Note that this must be
            frozen in an oven-proof pan.
    Serve with: Spinach salad, orange juice
Makes 6 to 8 servings

Baked Eggs

6 bread slices, cut into cubes
3 cups grated mild Cheddar cheese
1 cup cubed cooked ham
¼ cup chopped green pepper

½ cup chopped onion
6 eggs
3 cups milk

Combine all ingredients except the eggs and milk in a 13 × 9-inch baking dish. Whisk together the eggs and milk and pour over the top. Refrigerate overnight to serve tomorrow morning, or freeze the dish.

When thawed, bake, uncovered, at 375° F for 45 minutes.

Summary of processes
    Grate: 3 cups mild Cheddar cheese
    Chop: ¼ cup green pepper, ½ cup onion
    Freeze in: 13 × 9-inch baking dish
    Serve with: Sweet roll, grapefruit or orange slices

Note: This is also good substituting 6 slices cooked crumbled bacon for the ham.

Makes 8 to 10 servings

Barbecued Fillets

5 slices bacon
1 pound lean ground beef
Salt
Lemon pepper
¼ cup grated Parmesan cheese

1 2-ounce can mushroom stems and
  pieces, drained
1 tablespoon minced onion
2 tablespoons finely chopped green
  pepper

In a skillet or microwave cook bacon until limp, not crisp. Drain on paper towel. Pat the ground beef on waxed paper into a 12 × 8 × ¼-inch rectangle. Sprinkle lightly with salt and lemon pepper. Top with Parmesan cheese.

Combine the mushrooms, onion, and green pepper and sprinkle evenly over the meat. Roll up jelly-roll fashion, starting from the long side. Cut into 1½-inch wide slices.

Wrap the edge of each slice with a strip of partially cooked bacon, securing with wooden picks. Freeze with a piece of waxed paper between each patty.

When thawed, grill over medium coals 8 minutes. Turn and grill 8 more minutes.

Summary of processes
Mince: 1 tablespoon onion
Chop: 2 tablespoons green pepper
Freeze in: Large freezer bag
Serve with: Baked potatoes or Tater Tots, spinach salad
Makes 5 servings

Ravioli Soup

¼ cup soft bread crumbs
¼ cup grated Parmesan cheese
¾ teaspoon onion salt
2 cloves garlic, minced or pressed
1 pound lean ground beef, browned
  (2½ cups browned meat)
1 tablespoon olive oil or salad oil
1¾ cups finely chopped onion
1 28-ounce can tomatoes
1 6-ounce can tomato paste
1 14½-ounce can beef broth or
  bouillon
½ cup sherry

1 cup water
½ teaspoon *each* sugar and dried
  basil
¼ teaspoon *each* dried thyme and
  oregano
1 12-ounce package frozen ravioli
  (plain, without sauce), thawed
  (used on serving day)
¼ cup chopped fresh parsley (used on
  serving day)
Grated Parmesan cheese (used on
  serving day)

In a large pot combine all ingredients except the frozen ravioli, parsley, and additional Parmesan cheese. Chop the canned tomatoes as you stir ingredients. Bring to a boil, reduce heat, cover, and simmer 10 minutes. Freeze.

When thawed, bring the soup to a boil and then simmer, uncovered, at least 30 minutes. Cook the ravioli according to package directions until just tender. Drain the ravioli and add it to the soup. Salt to taste. Stir in parsley and serve with cheese to sprinkle over the thick soup.

Summary of processes
> *Mince:* 2 cloves garlic
> *Chop:* 1¾ cup onion, ¼ cup parsley
> *Freeze in:* 8-cup freezer container
> *Serve with:* Cole slaw or tossed salad and French bread

Makes 6 servings

Manicotti

1 8-ounce box manicotti	¼ teaspoon pepper
1 tablespoon vegetable oil	1 tablespoon chopped fresh parsley
1 15-ounce container Ricotta cheese	1 teaspoon salt
1 16-ounce container cottage cheese	2 eggs
1 cup grated mozzarella cheese	2 cups Spaghetti Sauce (page 42)
⅓ cup grated Parmesan cheese	

Boil the manicotti according to package directions, using 1 tablespoon oil in the water so they won't stick together.

Meanwhile, mix together all remaining ingredients except the spaghetti sauce.

Drain manicotti and run under cold water to cool it. Stuff each manicotti with the cheese mixture. Place them in the freezer container and pour the spaghetti sauce around the stuffed manicotti. Freeze.

When thawed, bake, covered, for 45 minutes at 350° F, then, uncovered, for 15 minutes more.

Summary of processes
> *Chop:* 1 tablespoon parsley
> *Grate:* 1 cup mozzarella cheese
> *Freeze in:* 3-quart casserole
> *Serve with:* Tossed salad and a combination of green beans, carrots, and
>   zucchini

Makes 8 servings

Taco Pie

1½ pounds lean ground beef (or 3¾ cups browned meat)

⅓ cup chopped onion (¼ cup sautéed onion)

1 envelope taco seasoning mix

1 4-ounce can diced green chilies, drained

2 cups milk

1 5.5-ounce packet Bisquick® baking mix (1⅓ cups)

4 eggs

1 cup grated Cheddar cheese

2 tomatoes, sliced (used on serving day)

Optional: Sour cream, chopped tomatoes, shredded lettuce (used on serving day)

Lightly grease 10-inch pie plate. Brown the ground beef with the onion. Drain. Combine these with the taco seasoning mix and spread in pie plate. Sprinkle with chilies.

Beat the milk, baking mix, and eggs until smooth, 15 seconds on high in a blender or 1 minute with hand beater. Pour into pie plate. Freeze with the grated cheese in a freezer bag attached to the side.

When thawed, bake, uncovered, 35 minutes at 400° F. Top with tomatoes and sprinkle with cheese. Bake until cheese is golden brown, 8 to 10 minutes longer. Top with sour cream, chopped tomatoes, and shredded lettuce if desired.

Summary of processes

Chop: ⅓ cup onion

Grate: 1 cup Cheddar cheese

Freeze in: 10-inch greased quiche or pie plate

Serve with: Guacamole dip with tortilla chips, fruit salad

Note: This pie may be a bit too large for the 10-inch pie plate. Put the overflow in a small container for a shut-in friend.

Makes 6 to 8 servings

Joes to Go

2 pounds lean ground beef (5 cups browned meat)

1½ cups chopped onion (1 cup sautéed onion)

1 clove minced garlic

1 teaspoon salt

⅛ teaspoon pepper

1 cup chili sauce

½ cup brown sugar

2 tablespoons vinegar

2 tablespoons mustard

2 8-ounce cans tomato sauce

12 hamburger buns (used on serving day)

Brown the ground beef with the onion in a large skillet. Drain. Add the remaining ingredients (except for the buns!) and simmer 10 minutes. Freeze in one or more containers. Freeze the hamburger buns.

When thawed, heat the mixture and serve warm on buns.

Summary of processes

    Chop: 1½ onion
    Mince: 1 clove garlic
    Freeze in: 8-cup freezer container
    Serve with: Potato chips and carrot and celery sticks

Note: For picnics or school or work lunches, take the hot meat sauce in a wide-mouth thermos so it can be eaten piping hot.

Makes enough to cover 12 buns

Cheesy Corn Casserole

1½ pounds lean ground beef (3¾ cups browned meat)
1 17-ounce can corn, drained
2 eggs, beaten slightly
1½ cups cottage cheese with chives, drained
1 tablespoon flour
1 8-ounce can tomato sauce
½ teaspoon minced garlic
¼ teaspoon cinnamon
½ cup grated Parmesan cheese (used on serving day)
1 cup grated mozzarella cheese (used on serving day)
½ cup slivered almonds (used on serving day)

Brown the ground beef and drain. Meanwhile spread the corn in the bottom of an 11×7-inch baking dish. Combine the eggs and cottage cheese and spread this mixture over the corn.

Stir the flour into the browned ground beef and cook 1 minute. Add the tomato sauce, garlic, and cinnamon. Layer the meat mixture on top of the cottage cheese and egg.

Freeze with the Parmesan, mozzarella, and almonds in freezer bags taped to the baking dish.

When thawed, sprinkle with the cheeses and nuts on top. Bake, uncovered, at 350° F for 30 minutes.

Summary of processes

    Mince: ½ teaspoon garlic
    Grate: 1 cup mozzarella cheese
    Freeze: 11×7-inch baking dish
    Serve with: Cornbread, beets, spinach salad

Makes 6 servings

(From left) Kindra, Kevin, Mimi, Kurt (kneeling) and Calvin Wilson

Month #2

Menu Calendar for
Month #2

SUN.	MON.	TUES.	WED.	THURS.	FRI.	SAT.
					1 Cooking Day Eat out!	**2** Cheese Soup
3 Salad Bowl Puff	**4** Pork Chops and Limas	**5** Deborah's Sweet and Sour Chicken	**6** French Stew (Company 8)	**7** Shish Kebabs	**8** Chicken and Rice Pilaf	**9** Roast Beef
10 Crustless Spinach Quiche	**11** Roast Beef Sandwiches or Hash	**12** Green Chili Enchiladas	**13** Chicken à la King (Luncheon 6)	**14** Sausage and Rice	**15** Eat Out	**16** Marinated Flank Steaks
17 Grandma's Chili	**18** Currant Ham Loaf	**19** Lasagne (Company 7)	**20** Eat Out	**21** Chicken Broccoli	**22** Balkan Meatballs	**23** BBQ Take Baked Beans & Hamburger
24 Zoo... Jan's Sans Ham Slices **31**	**25** Bird's Nest Pie	**26** Chicken Tetrazzini (Take half to Joan)	**27** Spicy Cabbage Rolls	**28** Eat Out	**29** Fish Fillets	**30** Eat Out

59

GROCERY SHOPPING LIST FOR MONTH #2

The following is a shopping list for the recipes in sample month #2. *It assumes the items given on the Pantry List are on hand.* An asterisk (*) after an item indicates it can be stored for use until the day its dish is served.

Canned

6 10¾-ounce cans cream of
  mushroom soup
3 10¾-ounce cans cream of chicken
  soup
1 10¾-ounce can beef consommé
2 6-ounce cans tomato paste
1 12-ounce can tomato paste
5 1-pound cans tomatoes
1 8-ounce can tomato sauce
1 15-ounce can tomato sauce
1 7-ounce can green chili salsa
1 4-ounce can diced green chilies
1 15-ounce can kidney beans
1 3-pound 5-ounce can pork and
  beans
1 8½-ounce can whole onions
1 16-ounce can small peas
1 16-ounce can whole green beans
2 8-ounce cans sliced water chestnuts
1 2-ounce jar pimiento
1 12-ounce can V8 juice
1 8-ounce can pineapple chunks
1 10-ounce jar currant jelly*
1 12-ounce can corned beef (*not*
  corned beef hash)
4 4-ounce cans sliced mushrooms
1 6-ounce jar prepared mustard*
Make sure you have 1¼ cups
  mayonnaise, 2 cups white wine,
  ¾ cup sherry, and ½ cup dry red
  wine on hand. These are on the
  Pantry List.

Dry

1 6½-ounce package Uncle Ben's Fast
  Cooking Long Grain and Wild
  Rice®
2 8-ounce packages spaghetti
1 8-ounce box lasagne
1 package onion soup mix
1 cup fine dry bread crumbs
8 buns or onion rolls
Croutons to make ¼ cup crumbs*
Make sure you have on hand at least
  1 cup raw rice and enough crackers
  to make 1 cup crumbs.

Frozen

2 packages Pepperidge Farm Patty
  Shells®*
1 10-ounce package chopped spinach
1 10-ounce package peas
1 10-ounce package lima beans
1 10-ounce package chopped broccoli

Dairy

2 sticks margarine or butter
  (1 stick*)
14 eggs (4*)
2 16-ounce containers cottage cheese
  (large curd)
1 8-ounce container cottage cheese
1 12-ounce container sour cream
1 8-ounce container sour cream
1¾ pounds Monterey Jack cheese
1¼ pounds mozzarella cheese

1¼ pounds mild Cheddar cheese
8 to 12 flour tortillas
1 8-ounce jar Cheez Whiz®
2 quarts milk (1½ quarts*)
1 pint half and half
Make sure you have on hand at least
    1¾ cups grated Parmesan cheese

Meat, Poultry, and Seafood
2 pounds cubed beef for kebabs
3 pounds stew meat
7 pounds lean ground beef
1 flank steak
8 loin pork chops
2½ pounds ground pork
1 8-ounce package bacon
2 pounds Italian sausage
6 to 7 pounds cooked ham (3 pounds
    ground, 1 pound cubed, and the
    center portion cut in dinner
    slices*)

13 pounds whole chickens *or* 11
    pounds chicken breasts only *plus* 4
    chicken breast halves
Beef roast*
Fish fillets*

Produce
10 onions (¾ cup chopped*)
5 green peppers
1 bunch green onions
6 carrots
1 apple
3 cloves garlic
1 bunch celery
1 large green cabbage
1 medium tomato (or use canned
    tomatoes)
Optional: Green pepper, canned
    onions, cherry tomatoes, and
    pineapple chunks for Shish Kebabs
    (page 77)

SUGGESTED FREEZER CONTAINERS FOR MONTH #2

Heavy aluminum foil
5 large freezer bags
1 6-cup freezer container
4 8-cup freezer containers
1 10-cup freezer container
1 12-cup freezer container

1 14-cup freezer container
1 loaf pan (or large freezer bag)
2 10-inch quiche or pie plates
1 11 × 7-inch baking dish
4 13 × 9-inch baking dishes

ASSEMBLY ORDER FOR MONTH #2

Day Before
1. Cook and debone all the chicken except the 4 breast halves. Wear rubber gloves if deboning chicken while it's hot.
2. Refrigerate chicken broth and chicken.
3. Freeze the buns or onion rolls and patty shells.

Night Before
1. Set out recipes, bowls, appliances, freezing containers, and canned and dry ingredients.
2. Start French Stew in the crockpot.

Begin Cooking Day
1. Cool and freeze the French Stew. Wash out the crockpot.
2. Mix 2 quarts milk from milk powder (optional).
3. Perform all the chopping, grating, slicing, and crushing necessary:
   Ham: Dice 2 cups if your butcher didn't do this.
   Onions: Chop 9 onions, 2 of them coarsely.
   Green onions: Chop 1 bunch.
   Green peppers: Chop 4½—1 of them in coarse pieces.
   Celery: Chop 2 cups, 1 of the cups in coarse pieces.
   Carrots: Slice 1 carrot, shred 2 carrots.
   Garlic: Mince 2 cloves.
   Mozzarella cheese: Slice 1¼ pounds.
   Monterey Jack cheese: Grate all 1¾ pounds.
   Mild Cheddar cheese: Grate all 1¼ pounds.
   Crumbs: Crush ½ cup fine dry bread crumbs, 1 cup cracker crumbs, ¼ cup crouton crumbs.
   Bacon: Dice ¼ pound + 3 strips (put in separate dishes).
   Apple: Chop 1 (Sprinkle with lemon juice or wait to chop until the apple is needed).
4. Brown together all but 1 pound of the ground beef.
5. Meanwhile, sauté together in butter or margarine 8½ cups onions.
6. Grease baking dishes that require it.
7. Skim fat from chicken broth and discard it.
8. Drain the browned ground beef and the sautéed onions. Set them aside.

Assemble Ground Beef Dishes

1. Assemble Grandma's Chili in the crockpot using browned ground beef and sautéed onions.
2. Combine the ingredients for the lasagne sauce and simmer in a saucepan while you boil the lasagne. Assemble Lasagne.
3. Assemble Baked Beans and Hamburger using browned ground beef and sautéed onions.
4. Assemble the Balkan Meatballs.
5. While the meatballs are broiling, assemble the Green Chili Enchiladas, using browned ground beef and sautéed onions.
6. Freeze the ground beef dishes.

Assemble Sausage Dishes

1. Brown all the sausage together and drain.
2. Cook the whole pound of spaghetti, reserving half of it for the Chicken Tetrazzini (toss the spaghetti with ½ tablespoon oil to prevent it from sticking together.)
3. Assemble Bird's Nest Pie, using sautéed onions.
4. Assemble Sausage and Rice using sautéed onions.
5. Freeze sausage dishes.

Assemble Chicken Dishes

1. Assemble Chicken Tetrazzini, using sautéed onions, and sauté the green pepper.
2. Assemble Deborah's Sweet and Sour Chicken.
3. Assemble Chicken à la King.
4. Assemble Chicken Broccoli.
5. Assemble Chicken and Rice Pilaf.
6. Freeze chicken dishes.

Assemble Ham Dishes

1. Separate the cabbage leaves carefully (for Spicy Cabbage Rolls) and boil them in the pot of chicken broth.
2. Assemble the Salad Bowl Puff.
3. Assemble Currant Ham Loaf.
4. Assemble Spicy Cabbage Rolls.
5. Freeze ham dishes.

Assemble Miscellaneous Dishes

1. Make Cheese Soup with 3½ cups of the remaining chicken broth. Let it simmer while you finish the last recipes.

2. While the pork chops are browning (Pork Chops and Limas), assemble Marinated Flank Steak and Shish Kebabs.
3. Assemble Pork Chops and Limas.
4. Assemble Crustless Spinach Quiche.
5. Assemble Jan's Sandwiches.
6. Freeze miscellaneous dishes.
7. Freeze Grandma's Chili.

Recipes for Month #2

French Stew

3 pounds stew meat
3 large carrots, sliced
1 8½-ounce can onions, drained
1 16-ounce can tomatoes
1 16-ounce can small peas, drained
1 10¾-ounce can beef consommé
1 16-ounce can whole green beans, drained

1 cup white wine
¼ cup minute tapioca
1 tablespoon brown sugar
½ cup fine dry bread crumbs
1 bay leaf
1 tablespoon salt
¼ teaspoon pepper

Combine all ingredients and bake in a covered large pot 6 to 8 hours at 250° F or in a large crockpot 8 to 10 hours on low. You could serve this to your family for dinner on cooking day, freezing what is left over.

Summary of processes
Slice: 3 large carrots
Freeze in: 14-cup freezer container
Serve with: Serve as is or over wild rice with gelatin salad and French bread
Makes 12 servings

Grandma's Chili

1 tablespoon olive oil
2 pounds lean ground beef (or 5 cups browned meat)
1½ cups chopped onion (or ¾ cup sautéed onion)
1 cup chopped green pepper
1 tablespoon Worcestershire sauce
¾ teaspoon chili powder

¼ teaspoon cinnamon
⅛ teaspoon garlic powder
Salt and black pepper to taste
1 15-ounce can tomato sauce
1 6-ounce can tomato paste
1 16-ounce can peeled tomatoes
1 15-ounce can kidney beans, drained

Heat oil in a large skillet over moderate heat. Crumble in beef. Cook till lightly brown, adding onions during the final minutes. Drain off grease. Add remaining ingredients. Simmer, covered, over low heat 2 hours or in crockpot on low 6 hours. Stir occasionally. Freeze.

When thawed, heat and serve. This is great in a thermos for the children's hot lunch!

Summary of processes
    Chop: 1½ cups onion, 1 cup green pepper
    Freeze in: 8-cup freezer container
    Serve with: Cornbread, fruit salad
Makes 12 servings

Lasagne

1 pound lean ground beef (or 2½ cups browned meat)
1 clove garlic, minced
1 tablespoon parsley flakes
1 tablespoon dried basil
1 teaspoon salt
1 16-ounce can tomatoes
1 12-ounce can tomato paste
1 8-ounce box lasagne

2 12-ounce containers large curd cottage cheese
2 eggs, beaten
1½ teaspoons salt
½ teaspoon pepper
2 tablespoons parsley flakes
½ cup grated Parmesan cheese
1 pound sliced mozzarella cheese

Brown meat and drain. Add the next 6 ingredients and simmer, uncovered, 30 minutes. Stir frequently. Cook the lasagne until bendable but not too soft. Combine the next 6 ingredients. In a greased 13 × 9-inch baking dish, layer half the lasagne, half the cottage cheese mixture, half the mozzarella, and half the beef sauce. Repeat the layers and freeze.

When thawed, bake, uncovered, at 375° F for 30 to 40 minutes.

Summary of processes
    Mince: 1 clove garlic
    Slice: 1 pound mozzarella cheese
    Freeze in: Greased 13 × 9-inch baking dish
    Serve with: Fresh broccoli or asparagus, fruit salad
Makes 8 servings

Baked Beans and Hamburger

¼ pound bacon, diced
1½ pounds lean ground beef (or 3¾ cups browned meat)
2½ cups chopped onions (or 1 cup sautéed onions)
1 3-pound 5-ounce can pork and beans in tomato sauce

1 pound can tomatoes, drained
½ cup brown sugar
½ cup catsup
Salt and pepper to taste

Brown bacon, ground beef, and onion. Drain grease. Combine all ingredients in a large container and freeze.

When thawed bake, uncovered, in large baking dish for 30 to 45 minutes at 350° F.

Summary of processes
> *Dice:* ¼ pound bacon
> *Chop:* 2½ cups onions
> *Freeze in:* 10-cup freezer container
> *Serve with:* Swedish Rye Bread (page 91), deviled eggs, gelatin salad

Makes 12 servings

Balkan Meatballs

1 egg
½ cup milk
½ cup fine dry bread crumbs
1 teaspoon *each* salt and sugar
¼ teaspoon *each* ground ginger, nutmeg, and allspice
1 pound lean ground beef
½ pound ground pork

1 cup finely chopped onion
4 tablespoons butter or margarine (used on serving day)
¼ cup flour (used on serving day)
2 cups milk (used on serving day)
Chopped parsley for garnish (used on serving day)

In a medium-size mixing bowl beat the egg with ½ cup milk. Blend in the bread crumbs, salt, sugar, and spices. Thoroughly mix in the ground meats and onion. Shape into meatballs about the size of walnuts. Place the meatballs on a cookie sheet and broil until lightly browned. (Use the timer to remind you they're in there.) Put into a freezer bag and freeze.

When thawed, add the flour to 4 tablespoons melted butter in a large skillet. Stir until bubbly and gradually add the milk, cooking over medium high till thick and smooth. Add the meatballs to the pan, cover, and simmer 15 minutes. Sprinkle with parsley.

Summary of processes
> *Chop:* 1 cup onion, parsley for garnish
> *Freeze in:* Large freezer bag
> *Serve with:* Thick egg noodles or rice, fresh broccoli, brownies

Makes 6 servings

Green Chili Enchiladas

1½ pounds lean ground beef (or 3¾ cups browned meat)
1¼ cups chopped onion (¾ cup sautéed)
1 tablespoon chili powder
Salt and pepper

8 to 12 flour tortillas
3 cups grated Monterey Jack cheese
1 10¾-ounce can cream of chicken soup
1½ cups sour cream
1 4-ounce can diced green chilies

Brown ground beef and sauté onions. Combine these with chili powder, salt, and pepper. Spoon enough meat mixture and cheese on each tortilla to cover ⅓ of the tortilla, reserving 1 cup of the cheese for the top.

Roll up each tortilla beginning with the filled edge. Place seam side down in greased 13 × 9-inch baking dish. When tortillas are completed, cover with a sauce made by combining the soup, sour cream, and chilies and freeze with the extra cheese in a bag taped to the baking dish.

When thawed, sprinkle remaining cheese on top and bake, uncovered, at 375° F for 20 to 25 minutes.

Summary of processes
Chop: 1¼ cups onion
Grate: 3 cups Monterey Jack cheese
Freeze in: Greased 13 × 9-inch baking dish
Serve with: Tossed green salad, avocado, tomato for color
Makes 8 servings

Bird's Nest Pie

1 8-ounce package spaghetti
2 eggs, beaten
⅓ cup grated Parmesan cheese
2 tablespoons butter (if you haven't already sautéed the onions)
½ cup chopped onion (or ¼ cup sautéed onion)

1 cup sour cream
1 pound Italian sausage (or 2½ cups browned meat)
1 6-ounce can tomato paste
1 cup water
4 ounces sliced mozzarella cheese

Break the spaghetti in half and cook it in boiling water until done. Drain. While it is still warm combine it with the eggs and Parmesan cheese. Pour into a well-greased pie plate and pat mixture up and around sides with a spoon. Melt butter and sauté onion until limp. Stir in sour cream and spoon over spaghetti.

Remove sausage from its casing, crumble, and brown in skillet. Drain. Add to it the tomato paste and water. Simmer 10 minutes. Spoon the sausage mixture on top of the sour cream mixture. Freeze with cheese in a freezer bag attached.

When thawed, bake, uncovered, at 350° F for 25 minutes. Arrange the mozzarella slices on top and return to the oven until the cheese melts.

Summary of processes
  Chop: ½ cup onion
  Slice: 4 ounces mozzarella cheese
  Freeze in: Greased 10-inch quiche or pie plate
  Serve with: Spinach salad, carrots and peas

Note: Try doubling this recipe and use 3 9-inch pie plates for a double recipe.

Makes 8 servings

Sausage and Rice

1 6¼-ounce box Uncle Ben's Fast Cooking Long Grain and Wild Rice®
1 pound Italian sausage
1¼ cups chopped onion
1 cup chopped green pepper

1 8-ounce can sliced water chestnuts, drained
1 cup chopped celery
1 4-ounce can sliced mushrooms
1 10¾-ounce can cream of mushroom soup
1 tablespoon salt

Cook the rice according to package directions and brown the sausage, draining well. Sauté the onion until tender. Mix all the ingredients together and freeze.

When thawed, bake 1 hour, uncovered, at 350° F.

Summary of processes
  Chop: 1¼ cups onion, 1 cup green pepper, 1 cup celery
  Freeze in: 8-cup freezer container *or* large freezer bag
  Serve with: Frozen salad, deviled eggs, and black olives

Note: This is quite spicy (and tasty!)—so it's not suitable for the ill.

Makes 6 servings

Chicken Tetrazzini

1 8-ounce package spaghetti
1¼ cups chopped onion
1 cup chopped green pepper
3 tablespoons butter (if you haven't already sautéed the onions)
5½ cups cooked, deboned, diced chicken

4 cups grated Monterey Jack cheese
2 10¾-ounce cans cream of mushroom soup
1 soup can milk
Salt and pepper to taste

Cook the spaghetti according to package directions. Sauté the onion and green pepper in the butter. Mix together all ingredients thoroughly in a large bowl. Freeze.

When thawed, bake, uncovered, at 350° F for 30 to 40 minutes, until bubbly.

Summary of processes
 Chop: 1 cup green pepper, 1¼ cups onion
 Grate: 4 cups Monterey Jack cheese
 Freeze in: 12-cup freezer container
 Serve with: Fruit salad, dinner roll
Makes 12 servings

Deborah's Sweet and Sour Chicken

1 cup sugar
3 tablespoons cornstarch
½ cup vinegar
Juice from 8-ounce can pineapple
 chunks
¼ cup soy sauce
½ teaspoon salt
1 clove garlic, minced
½ teaspoon paprika
½ teaspoon ginger

3 cups cooked, deboned, diced chicken
1 cup coarsely chopped onion
1 cup coarsely chopped celery
1 cup coarsely chopped green pepper
1 4-ounce can sliced mushrooms,
 drained
1 8-ounce can sliced water chestnuts,
 drained
1 8-ounce can pineapple chunks
 (reserve juice)

In a saucepan combine sugar and cornstarch, then add next 7 ingredients. Bring to a boil and simmer, stirring, until thickened. Pour in freezer container with chicken, fruit, and vegetables and freeze.

When thawed, bake, uncovered, for 45 minutes at 350 ° F.

Summary of processes
 Coarsely chop: 1 cup each onion, celery, green pepper
 Freeze in: 8-cup freezer container
 Serve with: Tossed green salad, white rice, pass soy sauce, dinner roll

Note: If you want to fill the house with a good aroma—this is the dish! Excellent using leftover cooked pork instead of chicken.

Makes 8 servings

Chicken à la King

3 strips bacon, diced
½ cup diced onion
1 4-ounce can sliced mushrooms
    (reserve ¼ cup liquid)
½ cup diced green pepper
2 tablespoons butter
½ cup all-purpose flour
2 teaspoons salt
½ teaspoon pepper

1 pint half and half
1⅓ cups chicken broth
¼ cup mushroom juice
1 tablespoon sherry
2 cups cooked, deboned, diced chicken
1 to 2 tablespoons pimiento (½ of a 2-ounce jar)
2 packages Pepperidge Farm Patty Shells® (used on serving day)

Sauté the bacon, onion, mushrooms, and green pepper in 2 tablespoons melted butter. Blend in flour, salt, and pepper and cook until bubbly.

Remove from heat and stir in half and half, chicken broth, ¼ cup mushroom juice, and sherry. Heat to boiling stirring constantly. Stir in the chicken and pimiento. Freeze.

When thawed, heat until bubbly and serve in patty shells.

Summary of processes
    Dice: 3 strips bacon, ½ cup onion, ½ cup green pepper
    Freeze in: Large freezer bag
    Serve with: Asparagus spears, red grapes
Makes 8 to 10 servings

Chicken Broccoli

1 10-ounce package frozen chopped broccoli
4 cups cooked, deboned, diced chicken
2 10¾-ounce cans cream of chicken soup
½ cup mayonnaise

1 4-ounce can sliced mushrooms
¼ teaspoon curry powder (more if you like curry)
3 tablespoons sherry
¾ cup grated Parmesan cheese

Cook the broccoli slightly in boiling water and spread it on the bottom of a greased 13 × 9-inch baking dish. Stir together the chicken, soup, mayonnaise, mushrooms, curry powder, sherry, and ½ cup of the Parmesan cheese and spread on top of the broccoli. Top with the remaining ¼ cup Parmesan cheese. Freeze.

When thawed, bake, covered, at 350° F for 40 minutes. Uncover and bake another 20 minutes.

Freeze in: Greased 13 × 9-inch baking dish
Serve with: Homemade bread, Cranberry Cream Salad (page 97)
Makes 6 to 8 servings

Chicken and Rice Pilaf

4 chicken breast halves (skin them
    with kitchen scissors)
Salt, pepper, paprika
1¼ cups water or chicken broth
1 cup raw rice
½ envelope dry onion soup mix (¼
    cup)

1 10¾-ounce can cream of mushroom
    soup
2 tablespoons pimiento (½ of a
    2-ounce jar)
¼ cup sherry

Season the chicken breasts with salt, pepper, and paprika. Combine the remaining ingredients and place in the bottom of a greased 11 × 7-inch baking dish. Put the chicken breasts on top and freeze.

When thawed, bake, uncovered, at 375° F for 1¼ hours, or until chicken and rice are tender.

Summary of processes
    Freeze in: Greased 11 × 7-inch baking dish
    Serve with: Marinated Veggies (page 96), dinner rolls
Makes 4 servings

Salad Bowl Puff

Ham Salad Filling
1 10-ounce package frozen peas
2 cups cubed cooked ham
1 cup grated Cheddar cheese
2 tablespoons minced onion

1½ teaspoons mustard
¾ cup mayonnaise (used on serving
    day)

Rinse the peas under cold water to separate but not thaw; drain. Combine the peas with all other ingredients except the mayonnaise. Freeze.

When thawed add the mayonnaise to the ham salad filling and make the following pastry:

Pastry (used on serving day)
⅔ cup water
¼ cup margarine

1 cup Bisquick®
4 eggs

Heat oven to 400° F. Generously grease 9-inch pie plate. Heat water and margarine to boiling in a 2-quart saucepan. Add Bisquick® all at once. Stir vigorously over low heat until the mixture forms a ball, about 1½ minutes. Remove from heat. Beat in eggs one at a time and continue beating until smooth. Spread mixture in pie pan (*not* up sides). Bake, uncovered, until puffed and dry in center, 35 to 40 minutes. Cool. Just before serving fill with cold ham salad filling.

Summary of processes
    Grate: 1 cup cheddar cheese
    Mince: 2 tablespoons onion
    Freeze in: Large freezer bag
    Serve with: Lemon gelatin salad with carrots and crushed pineapple
Makes 8 servings

Currant Ham Loaf

5 cups ground cooked ham
1 pound ground pork
2 eggs
1 cup cracker crumbs
1 8-ounce can tomato sauce
2 tablespoons chili sauce (use catsup
   if you don't have on hand)

1 10-ounce jar currant jelly (used on
   serving day)
½ 6-ounce jar mustard (used on
   serving day)

Combine all the ingredients except the jelly and mustard and form into a loaf. Freeze.

When thawed bake, uncovered, in a loaf pan for 1½ hours at 350° F. Stir together the jelly and mustard and pour over the loaf.

Summary of processes
    Crumb: 1 cup cracker crumbs
    Freeze in: Loaf pan *or* large freezer bag
    Serve with: Sweet potatoes glazed with orange juice and brown sugar,
            broccoli and cauliflower
Makes 6 servings

Spicy Cabbage Rolls

1 large green cabbage
1 pound ground pork
2 cups ground cooked ham
1 egg
¼ teaspoon salt
⅛ teaspoon *each* ground allspice,
  dillweed, pepper
2 tablespoons butter or margarine,
  melted

1 medium carrot, sliced
1 medium tomato, chopped (may use
  canned)
1½ cups finely chopped onion
1 cup dry white wine
1 12-ounce can V8 juice
Flour

Carefully remove and separate the cabbage leaves and boil them in the chicken broth on the stove until tender. (Save nutrients!) Stir together the ground pork, ground ham, egg, salt, allspice, dillweed, and pepper.

Combine in a separate bowl the butter, carrot, tomato, onion, wine, and V8. Wrap 2 tablespoons of the meat mixture into each cabbage leaf, roll up the leaf, and roll the leaf in flour. Arrange the rolled leaves on the bottom of a 13 × 9-inch baking dish. Pour the vegetable mixture over the cabbage rolls. Freeze.

When thawed, bake, covered, at 375° F for 1 hour. Uncover for the last 15 minutes.

Summary of processes
  Slice: 1 medium carrot
  Chop: 1 tomato, 1½ cups onion
  Freeze in: 13 × 9-inch baking dish
  Serve with: On a bed of rice with a scoop of sour cream on top (optional).
            A molded fruit salad and French-cut green beans add color.
Makes 8 to 10 servings

Cheese Soup

3½ cups chicken broth
2 carrots, shredded
1 cup cooked, deboned, diced chicken
3 tablespoons sherry
1 teaspoon Worcestershire sauce
⅓ teaspoon celery seed
2 cups grated mild Cheddar cheese

¾ cup chopped onion (used on serving
  day)
4 tablespoons butter or margarine
  (used on serving day)
¼ cup all-purpose flour (used on
  serving day)
4 cups milk (used on serving day)

In a large saucepan combine the first 6 ingredients. Bring to a boil and simmer, covered, for 1 hour. Freeze with the cheese in a freezer bag taped to the soup container.

When thawed, sauté onion in the butter. Add flour and milk to make a white sauce. Add the cheese to the white sauce to melt it. Add this sauce to the soup and heat through.

Summary of processes
Shred: 2 carrots
Grate: 2 cups mild Cheddar cheese
Freeze in: 1 8-cup freezer container
Serve with: Egg salad sandwiches, celery sticks
Makes 4 servings

Marinated Flank Steak

½ cup vegetable oil
¼ cup soy sauce
¼ cup sherry
2 teaspoon Worcestershire sauce

½ teaspoon ginger
1 minced clove garlic
1 flank steak

Combine all ingredients except the flank steak. Pour over the flank steak in a freezer bag and freeze with the flank steak in the marinade.

When thawed, remove the flank steak from the marinade and barbecue or broil it 8 to 12 minutes per side. Slice it against the grain thinly, cutting diagonally.

Summary of processes
Mince: 1 clove garlic
Freeze in: Large freezer bag
Serve with: Twice-Baked Potatoes Deluxe (page 95), peas, Frozen Fruit
     Medley (page 97)
Makes 4 servings

Shish Kebabs

2 pounds beef, cubed
1 7-ounce can green chili salsa
1½ cups coarsely chopped onion
1 tablespoon chili powder

2 tablespoons vegetable oil
½ cup dry red wine
¼ teaspoon salt
Pepper to taste

Combine all ingredients and pour into freezing container. Freeze.

When thawed (it can marinate while it thaws), skewer the meat with vegetables and barbecue or broil. Baste with marinade while cooking.

Summary of processes

Chop: 1½ cups onion coarsely
Freeze in: 6-cup freezer container *or* large freezer bag
Serve with: Suggested fruits and vegetables for skewer: green pepper strips, onions, cherry tomatoes, fresh mushrooms, pineapple chunks. Serve on a bed of steamy rice with a green salad and corn on the cob

Makes 8 servings

Pork Chops and Limas

8 loin pork chops
1 10-ounce package frozen lima beans
1 large apple, chopped

2 10¾-ounce cans cream of
   mushroom soup
1 teaspoon dried sage
Salt and pepper to taste

Brown pork chops in large skillet. Drain and cool on paper towel. Meanwhile run cold water over the lima beans to separate them (do not thaw them). Mix together all ingredients except the pork chops and place in freezer bag. Add chops to the freezer bag and freeze.

When thawed, bake, covered, at 350 ° F for 1 hour.

Summary of processes

Chop: 1 large apple
Freeze in: Large freezer bag
Serve with: Mashed potatoes (don't waste that good gravy) and spicy apple sauce

Makes 4 to 8 servings, depending on size of pork chops

Crustless Spinach Quiche

1 10-ounce package chopped frozen
 spinach
1 bunch green onions, chopped
4 eggs

1 16-ounce container cottage cheese
2 cups grated Cheddar cheese
¼ cup crouton crumbs (used on
 serving day)

Cook spinach according to package directions and squeeze to remove liquid. Combine with other ingredients, reserving the crouton crumbs for the top. Pour into a quiche pan or 10-inch pie plate. Freeze with crouton crumbs in a freezer bag attached to the side.

When thawed, bake, uncovered, 1 hour at 325° F, adding the crouton crumbs the last 15 minutes.

Summary of processes
    Chop: 1 bunch green onions
    Grate: 2 cups Cheddar cheese
    Crush: 4 tablespoons croutons
    Freeze in: 10-inch quiche pan or pie plate
    Serve with: Fresh sliced tomatoes and soft dinner rolls
Makes 8 servings

Jan's Sandwiches

1 12-ounce can corned beef (*not*
 corned beef hash)
1 8-ounce jar Cheez Whiz®
Small amount of chopped onion

Enough mayonnaise to moisten and
 hold mixture together
8 buns or onion rolls

Mix all ingredients and spread on buns. Wrap buns individually in foil and freeze.

When thawed, bake in foil 20 minutes at 350° F.

Summary of processes
    Chop: Small amount of onion
    Freeze in: Freeze individually wrapped in foil
    Serve with: Chips, pineapple and melon balls with honey dressing
Makes 8 servings

(From left) Daniel, Mary Beth, Drew, Tim, and Alex Lagerborg

Appendix

EQUIVALENTS

1 pound lean ground beef or sausage browned = 2½ cups

1 pound ground ham = 2½ cups

1 pound cubed ham = 3 cups

1 cooked, deboned whole chicken (about 4 pounds) = 4½ cups

1 cooked, deboned whole chicken (about 5 pounds) = 6 cups

1 medium yellow onion, chopped = 1¼ cups

1 medium yellow onion, chopped and sautéed = ¾ cup

1 medium green pepper, chopped = 1 cup

1 pound cheese, grated = 4 cups

FREEZING TIPS

Frozen foods keep their natural color, flavor, and nutritive qualities better than canned or dried foods. Freezing stops the bacterial action in food, but merely retards the food's enzyme action, or natural deterioration. Food kept in the freezer too long may not taste quite right, but it shouldn't make you sick.

Do . . .
- Freeze food quickly to 0 degrees F or below.
- Use the frozen food within a month to six weeks.
- If you use a home freezer, post a list of food on the freezer and keep it up to date.
- Thaw, heat, and serve in rapid succession.
- Before thawing baked goods, remove from the package and cover lightly with foil. Otherwise thaw foods in their original packaging.
- Bring foods to room temperature before freezing.
- When possible, thaw in the refrigerator or microwave. Thawing in the refrigerator will take twice as long as thawing on the countertop. Thawing time will vary with the thickness or quantity of food in the container.
- Freeze in moisture-proof, vapor-proof containers with an airtight seal. Use a straw to suck out all the air.

Good: glass (leave headspace), metal, rigid plastic, heavy aluminum foil, bags and wraps advertised for freezing.
Poor: regular waxed paper; lightweight aluminum foil; cartons for cottage cheese, ice cream, or milk; ordinary butcher paper or the plastic film used on packaged meats; plastic produce bags from the supermarket; cellophane.

Don't . . .
- Refreeze.
- Freeze the following. They will change color, texture, or separate in some way during freezing or thawing:

  Raw salad vegetables (such as lettuce, radishes, tomatoes).
  Raw eggs in their shells or hard-cooked eggs.
  Raw potatoes or boiled white potatoes.

Gelatin salads or desserts.
Icing made with egg whites, boiled frostings, or cakes with cream fillings.
Macaroni, some rice.
Mayonnaise (alone or on bread).
Custard pies, cream pies, or pies with meringue.

HELPFUL HINTS

- Use store-bought pie crusts and pastry shells or ones you've made ahead. Pastry is too lengthy (and messy) a process to attempt on cooking day.
- When you scan your favorite recipes to see if they would lend themselves well to this process, ask yourself these questions:

    1. Do all the ingredients freeze well?
    2. Does the recipe involve particularly complicated or time-consuming processes? If so forget it.
    3. Does the recipe necessitate taking up more than one or two burners at a time?
    4. Does the recipe require thawing any frozen ingredients? If so, you could not freeze the dish without cooking it.

- If you have a crockpot and use it overnight for brisket, you might want to wash it out and use it for a stew or soup on cooking day. There's one more dish for the freezer (or dinner that night) without using up stove space.
- If both you and your husband work and he helps with the cooking, try this as a project together one Saturday a month.
- If you will be sautéing several items in succession, use the same skillet. Rinsing will not always be necessary between uses.
- If you have leftover chopped onion, green pepper, chicken, etc., freeze them each in a freezer bag and use as needed.
- If you do not have a separate freezer, the trick is to use freezer bags or stacking containers whenever possible. If you do run out of freezer space toward the end of your cooking, decide which dishes you could eat within the next few days and put them in the refrigerator
- Mark the foods which you don't freeze, but which you'll need on hand when you serve your frozen dishes. This will remind you not to use them unwittingly. Mark an X in black marker across a soup label, for example, or store a needed fresh tomato in a plastic bag marked with an X.
- If you are shopping with children, try to break up the trip. For example, go to a discount food store for canned and dry foods mid-morning, then to a favorite fast food haunt for lunch, and afterward to your neighborhood supermarket to finish shopping.
- Remember to slightly undercook rice and noodles that will be frozen cooked.
- Try substituting turkey in the chicken recipes.
- Use an electric skillet on cooking day as an additional burner.

SAVING MORE MINUTES WITH THE HOME COMPUTER

If you own a home computer, this book may be the impetus you've needed to make it work for you in the kitchen.

A standard software package would allow you to enter a recipe program of all your favorite recipes. If you keep your Pantry List on the computer as well, you can use the computer to call forth a monthly Grocery Shopping List. Once a month ask the computer to search for the items you've entered throughout the preceding month as needed on the Pantry List. Then tell the computer what recipes you'll use that month and ask it to search for all the ingredients you'll need. Add your breakfast, lunch, and snack needs to the list and you're ready to go to market.

If you are able to program and have a more sophisticated software package, you could ask the computer to search and bring up which of your ground beef recipes, for example, have more than four ingredients in common. Or you could ask it to find—of the recipes you've chosen for that month—how many total onions to chop and how many total cups of Cheddar cheese to grate.

You could also program seasonal items and recipes. Then you would ask the computer to find the recipes that use items of the appropriate season, such as squash, apple, and cranberry recipes in the fall.

SCHOOL LUNCHES

Are you tired of paying for school lunches? Or tired of making them each day? Let me share an idea with you that has proved a boon in our household.

We have a ten-year-old daughter, Kindra, who is very creative but needs a little incentive. We also have a thirteen-year-old son, Kurt, and both of them need school lunches each week day. If they both bought them daily it would cost us $50.00 per month.

Each month we give Kindra $35.00 (on paper) with which to buy the ingredients for her and Kurt's lunches.* She makes her lists and menus, keeps her own records, and clips coupons. Once a month Kindra and I go grocery shopping with her coupons and lists. When we get home I help her prepare and freeze sandwiches and cookies. She packs their lunches before school each morning.

If Kindra spends under $35.00 on lunches for the month, she likes to save up and take the family out for dinner on what she's saved us. And if Kurt complains too much about the lunches, he has to fix them himself.

*This does not include beverages. Our children drink water at school, and then we make sure they get plenty of milk and juice at home.

BREAD BAKING

I enjoy baking and freezing breads and rolls, but *never* on cooking day. Usually I bake each Monday. One Monday I may bake whole-wheat bread and rolls and the next week raisin bread and muffins. Each week I make the scraps of dough into cinnamon rolls and dinner rolls. This gives me a variety of breads in my freezer at any one time.

I always bake the loaves before freezing them and I package them carefully for the freezer. One hole in the foil around the bread could cause it to dry out quickly.

Whenever possible I use honey instead of sugar. It's better for us and helps keep the bread moist.

Some of my favorite bread and muffin recipes are included here in case you're looking for some ideas.

Mimi's Nutritious Bread

1 package active dry yeast
3 cups lukewarm water
1 cup powdered milk (*not* made up)
½ cup honey
4 cups whole-wheat flour (1 cup can
  be wheat germ)

1½ tablespoons salt
½ cup vegetable oil
5 to 6 cups all-purpose flour
Melted butter or margarine

In a large mixing bowl dissolve the yeast in the water. Add the milk and honey, then the 4 cups whole-wheat flour. Beat with a whisk until lumps disappear (it will no thicker than dough for a cake). Let the dough rise 60 minutes.

Add the salt, oil, and white flour, working in all the flour the dough will take—until it's not sticky. Knead 3 to 4 minutes, until the dough is smooth. Put the dough into a large greased bowl and turn it once so it's greased on both top and bottom. Cover the top with a towel. Let it rise 50 minutes. Punch down and let rise 40 more minutes.

Shape into 2 large smooth loaves and put them in loaf pans which have been greased with shortening. Let rise in the pans, covered with a towel, 30 minutes. Set the timer for 15 minutes to remind yourself to preheat the oven to 350° F.

Bake 1 hour. When right out of the oven brush the top with melted butter or margarine.

89

Optional: Bake 1 loaf. Roll the other half of the dough into a long tube about 2 inches thick. Cut the tube at 2-inch intervals and roll the pieces into round rolls. Bake on a cookie sheet at 350° F for 25 to 30 minutes. Rub a cube of butter over the tops of the warm rolls.

Optional: Take the unbaked round rolls from above and flatten them into circles about the size of your palm. Fold each circle of dough around a small wedge of Cheddar cheese and 2 tablespoons browned ground beef. Bake sealed-side down on a cookie sheet 25 to 30 minutes at 350° F. Serve with barbecue sauce in a small container for dipping. Great for lunch.

Makes 2 loaves

Portuguese Sweetbread

2 packages active dry yeast
1⅔ cups warm water
1 cup dry instant potato flakes
1 cup sugar
6 tablespoons butter or margarine, melted
2 teaspoons salt
4 eggs

1 tablespoon finely shredded lemon or orange peel, or half of each
1½ cups raisins (half black and half golden)
7½ cups all-purpose flour
For Christmas, soak the raisins in 2 tablespoons rum

In a large mixing bowl soften the yeast in warm water. Add potato flakes, sugar, melted butter, salt, eggs, peel, and raisins. Mix well. Add all the flour necessary for the dough not to be sticky, approximately 7½ cups. Knead the dough 2 to 3 minutes. Put it into a large greased bowl and turn it once so that the dough is greased on top and bottom. Cover the top with a towel. If it's a cold day put the bowl on the dryer or by a heat vent.

Let it rise 1½ hours. Punch it down and let it rise another 10 minutes.

Divide the dough into 3 large round loaves or 4 smaller ones and place them on a greased cookie sheet with space between them. You can braid the dough or put it into any shape.

Cover the dough and let it rise until almost double—45 minutes. Bake the loaves at 350° F for 40 minutes. Cover them with foil after the first 20 minutes so they won't get too brown.

We give these festive loaves to our neighbors each Christmas.

This makes *great* toast with butter.

Makes 3 to 4 loaves

Spicy Pumpkin Muffins

1½ cups unsifted all-purpose flour
½ cup sugar
2 teaspoons baking powder
¾ teaspoon salt
1 teaspoon ground cinnamon
½ teaspoon ground ginger

¼ teaspoon ground cloves
½ cup raisins
1 egg
½ cup milk
½ cup canned pumpkin
¼ cup salad oil

Topping
2½ teaspoons sugar
½ teaspoon ground cinnamon

In a large mixing bowl stir together the flour, sugar, baking powder, salt, and spices until well combined. Mix in the raisins to coat well with flour mixture. In a smaller bowl beat the egg with milk, pumpkin, and oil.

Stir the egg mixture, all at once, into the flour mixture, mixing only until combined. Fill greased or nonstick muffin pans ⅔ full. Sprinkle with the sugar and cinnamon mixed together. Bake in a 400° F oven for 20 to 25 minutes, until nicely browned. Serve warm.

Makes 12 muffins

Swedish Rye Bread

2 packages dry yeast
¼ cup plus 1 teaspoon white sugar
9½ cups all-purpose flour
1 cup warm water
2 cups milk
1 cup water
5 tablespoons soft margarine

½ cup brown sugar
½ cup molasses
1 tablespoon salt
1¼ teaspoon anise seed
2 teaspoons caraway seed
3 cups rye flour
3 tablespoons dark corn syrup

Combine the yeast, 1 teaspoon white sugar, 1½ cups all-purpose flour, and 1 cup warm water in a small bowl; cover and let rise for about 30 minutes.

In a small saucepan scald the milk and 1 cup water mixed together. While scalding, in a large bowl put the margarine, brown sugar, ¼ cup white sugar, molasses, salt, anise seed, caraway seed, another 1 cup all-purpose flour, rye flour, and corn syrup.

Pour the scalded liquid on top of the mixture and stir. Pour in the yeast mixture and stir.

Add about 3 cups all-purpose flour gradually until a ball forms (use your hands). Then turn onto a bread board and gradually mix in 4 more cups. Put back into *greased* bowl and let rise until double.

Turn the dough back onto the bread board and divide into loaves. Use 3 or 4 greased loaf pans or shape into 5 or 6 small loaves on a cookie sheet.

Let the loaves rise about 45 minutes, then bake at 325° F for approximately 50 minutes. Rub a butter cube over the tops of the warm loaves. Remove from pans immediately and cool.

Note: These loaves are excellent as an alternative to cookies and fudge as Christmas gifts.

Makes 3 to 4 regular loaves or 5 to 6 small loaves.

The following recipes are favorites, added just for fun.

Miscellaneous Recipes

Orange Spiced Tea

2 cups Tang® orange drink mix
¾ cup instant tea mix
1 teaspoon cinnamon

1 teaspoon cloves
1 large package Wylers® lemonade
(pouch)

Mix all together. Stir 1 heaping teaspoon of mix into cup of hot water or glass water. Add more to taste. Great hot or cold and makes *lots*.

Cranberry Tea

1 cup cranberry juice
3 cups prepared iced tea

3 tablespoons lemon juice
¼ cup sugar

Combine all ingredients in a pitcher and chill.

Makes 1 quart

Homemade Yogurt

You will need 1 large Pyrex® mixing bowl and 3 quart jars with lids.

1 envelope unflavored gelatin
6 cups water
1 tablespoon sugar
3 cups powdered milk

1 13-ounce can evaporated milk
3 tablespoons plain yogurt
2 teaspoons vanilla (optional)

Soften the gelatin in ½ cup of the water. Then add enough boiling water to make 1 cup. Add the sugar and let the mixture cool.

Preheat the oven to 275° F. Mix 3 cups powdered milk with 3 cups water. Combine the evaporated milk, 2 more cups of tepid water and the gelatin mixture. Add the yogurt and flavoring and stir thoroughly.

Pour into 3 quart jars, but leave the lids off. Turn off the oven and place the jars inside it. Leave them there overnight (8 to 10 hours). In the morning put the lids on the jars.

Makes 2½ quarts

Ham Dinner Slices

¾-inch thick cooked ham slices   Brown sugar
Prepared mustard   Milk

Place the ham slices in a single layer in the bottom of a baking dish. Spread prepared mustard on the top of each slice and sprinkle brown sugar over the mustard. Pour enough milk over the ham slices to come half way up their sides. Bake 1 hour at 350° F uncovered.

Note: You can also dress up ham slices by rolling them around asparagus or broccoli spears and covering with cheese sauce.

Green Rice

1 egg, beaten   2 cups cooked rice
1 cup milk   1 teaspoon celery seed
½ cup chopped fresh parsley   ½ teaspoon curry powder
1 clove garlic, chopped   Salt to taste
1 small onion, minced

Mix all ingredients and bake in a greased dish or mold at 325° F for 30 to 40 minutes.

Makes 8 servings

Lemon Rice

1 cup raw white rice   ¼ cup margarine
1½ cups boiling water   ¾ cup heavy cream, slightly warmed
¼ teaspoon salt   2 tablespoons chopped fresh parsley
Juice and peel of 1 lemon

Add rice to boiling salted water. Simmer, covered, until the liquid is absorbed—about 20 minutes.

While the rice is cooking, sauté grated lemon peel in margarine for 3 minutes. Remove approximately ¾ of the lemon peel and discard. Pour the margarine and the remaining lemon peel over the rice. Gently toss in the lemon juice and warmed cream.

Empty into an ovenproof serving dish and keep rice warm in the oven until serving time. Garnish with parsley.

Note: Wonderful with fish.

Makes 6 servings

Twice-Baked Potatoes Deluxe

6 baking potatoes
Salt and pepper
Butter or margarine
Milk
¼ cup chopped onion

¾ cup grated Cheddar cheese
¾ cup grated Monterey Jack cheese
1 box frozen chopped spinach, thawed
  and pressed dry

Bake the 6 potatoes. While still hot, slice each potato in half lengthwise and carefully scoop the baked potato into a large mixing bowl. Save the skins.

Mix the potatoes with the remaining ingredients, using salt, pepper, and butter to taste and enough milk for desired "mashed potato" consistency. Put the potato mixture back into the skins.

Serve immediately or freeze them in a freezer bag. Remove as needed and heat on a cookie sheet or flat baking dish.

Makes 12 servings

Bread and Butter Pickles

20 3-inch long cucumbers, sliced
½ cup salt
Ice
6 onions, sliced
1 quart vinegar
4 cups sugar

1 tablespoon celery seed
2 tablespoons mustard seed
1 tablespoon ground ginger
1 teaspoon ground turmeric
  (optional)
½ teaspoon white pepper

Slice the cucumbers. Add salt and stir gently. Cover with ice for about 3 hours, replacing ice as needed.

Drain cucumbers and rinse off salt. Add onions. Run 8 1-pint canning jars through the dishwasher. Boil the lids and tongs. Heat water to boiling in a water-bath kettle.

Meanwhile boil together the vinegar, sugar, and spices for 10 minutes. Add the cucumbers and onions and bring to the boiling point.

Fill the jars, seal them, and process in the water bath for 15 minutes.

Makes 8 pints

Marinated Veggies

Mix together any four of your favorite canned vegetables (drained), for example, four of the following:

Artichoke hearts	Beets
Olives	Julienne carrots
Green beans	Whole tomatoes

Add to these the following:

Fresh mushrooms, sliced

Fresh broccoli, steamed till crisp-tender

In a separate bowl mix:

1 cup cider vinegar	¾ teaspoon dried oregano
1 cup salad oil	¾ teaspoon salt
1 large garlic clove, minced	¼ teaspoon pepper
¾ teaspoon dried basil	½ small onion, minced

Bring the marinade to a boil and simmer for 10 minutes. Toss the veggies in the marinade and refrigerate for several hours.

Toss your favorite small pasta with leftovers for a Presto Pasta Salad.

Jiffy Salad

1 small head lettuce	2 tablespoons vinegar
2 to 3 hard-cooked eggs, chopped	1 teaspoon soy sauce
¼ teaspoon salt	1 tablespoon chopped fresh parsley
¼ teaspoon pepper	¼ cup grated Parmesan cheese
¼ cup oil	

Shred the lettuce, top with hard-cooked eggs, and toss with the other ingredients whisked together for a dressing.

Cranberry Cream Salad

1 cup heavy cream
3 tablespoons sugar
2 3-ounce packages cream cheese
1 16-ounce can whole cranberry
   sauce

1 8-ounce can crushed pineapple,
   drained

Whip the cream. Add the sugar, then the other ingredients. Pour into a loaf pan and freeze.

To serve, thaw slightly and slice into pieces. May be served as a dessert or a salad on lettuce leaves.

Makes 8 to 10 servings

Frozen Fruit Medley

1 17-ounce can apricots
1 20-ounce can crushed pineapple
1 cup liquid drained from apricots
   and pineapple
½ cup sugar
2 16-ounce packages frozen
   strawberries, partially thawed and
   broken up

1 6-ounce can frozen orange juice
   concentrate
2 tablespoons lemon juice
3 bananas, diced

Drain apricots and pineapple, reserving 1 cup of the combined liquid. Heat the liquid and sugar, stirring until the sugar dissolves. Combine the liquid with the apricots, pineapple, and remaining ingredients. Spoon into cupcake papers put in muffin tins. Freeze until sold.

When frozen turn over the muffin tins and punch out the frozen fruit cups with your thumb. Package the frozen fruit cups in freezer bags. Remove them from the freezer 20 minutes before serving to partially thaw.

Makes 30 servings

Fresh Baked Asparagus

1 to 1½ pounds fresh asparagus
Salt and pepper (lemon pepper, if
   desired)

3 tablespoons butter

Rinse and trim the stumps off the asparagus. Place it in one or two layers in flat baking pan. Sprinkle with salt and pepper and dot with butter. Cover with foil and bake 30 minutes at 300° F. The asparagus will be crunchy and not lose color.

Makes 6 to 8 servings

Hot Spiced Fruit

1 16-ounce can sliced peaches with
  liquid
1 17-ounce can pears with liquid
1 15-ounce can pineapple chunks
  with liquid

½ cup orange marmalade
1 3-inch cinnamon stick
½ teaspoon ground nutmeg
¼ teaspoon ground cloves

Mix together all these ingredients, with the fruits undrained. Simmer for 1 hour. Try fixing in a crockpot. Imagine the aroma!

This is good with sliced ham. Try it as a sauce over ice cream.

Makes 12 servings

Smoky Corn Chowder

½ cup chopped onions
4 tablespoons butter or margarine
¼ cup all-purpose flour
1¼ teaspoons salt
¼ teaspoon pepper

4 cups milk
1 16-ounce can whole-kernel corn,
  drained
8 smoked sausage links, sliced
1 8-ounce can lima beans (optional)

In a saucepan sauté the onion in butter till tender but not brown. Blend in the flour, salt, and pepper. Add the milk all at once. Bring to boiling and stir till thick and bubbly, about a minute.

Stir in the corn, sausage, and lima beans. Reduce heat and simmer 10 minutes.

Makes 6 servings

Auntie Teeto's Waffles

This recipe was given to me by my ninety-four-year-old aunt, who used an equally old waffle iron.

2 cups all-purpose flour (try using a
   little whole-wheat or buckwheat
   flour for part of the flour)
1 teaspoon baking soda

1 teaspoon salt
1½ cups buttermilk
2 eggs, lightly beaten
2 tablespoons salad oil

Sift together flour, soda, and salt. In a separate bowl, combine buttermilk, eggs, and oil. Add liquid ingredients to dry ingredients, stirring just to moisten. Pour batter into the center of a greased waffle iron. Cook a minute or two until the iron "smokes." Serve with warmed maple syrup.

Makes 6 servings

Good Day Granola

8 cups rolled oats (not instant)
1¼ cups firmly packed brown sugar
1½ cups unprocessed bran
1½ cups natural wheat germ (not
   toasted or honeyed)
¾ cup chopped walnuts

½ cup raw sunflower seeds
½ cup vegetable oil
¾ cup honey
2 teaspoons vanilla
2 cups raisins

Stir together first six ingredients. In a small pan over medium heat stir the oil, honey, and vanilla till bubbly. Thoroughly mix together the liquid and dry ingredients.

Divide the mixture evenly on two rimmed cookie sheets. Bake at 325° F 15 to 20 minutes, stirring once to keep the granola evenly browned. While it cools, stir the mixture several times to keep it from sticking together.

When thoroughly cool, add raisins. Store in airtight container.

Note: Keeps for weeks and is yummy for breakfast or snacks.

Makes about 12 cups

Cinnamon Logs

2 egg yolks
1¾ cups sugar
2 8-ounce packages cream cheese, at room temperature

3 loaves Pepperidge Farm sandwich bread
4 sticks margarine, melted
4 teaspoons cinnamon

Mix together the egg yolks and ½ cup sugar, then add the cream cheese. Trim the crusts from the bread and roll each slice with a rolling pin to flatten it.

Spread the cheese mixture on a slice of bread. Put a slice on top to make a sandwich. Cut each sandwich into 4 logs lengthwise. Stir together the cinnamon and remaining 1¼ cups sugar.

Dip each log in the melted margarine, then the cinnamon/sugar mixture. Freeze the logs on cookie sheets. When they're frozen, package them in freezer bags.

To serve take as many as you want to serve from the freezer bag and put them *still frozen* on a cookie sheet or flat baking dish. Bake at 400° F for 10 minutes.

Makes 80 to 100 logs

Blueberry Pie

1 10-ounce jar currant jelly
1 pint box fresh blueberries

1 graham cracker crust, baked
1 pint sour cream

Melt the jelly in a saucepan over low heat. Add the blueberries and stir. Pour into the graham cracker crust.

Spread sour cream on top and refrigerate overnight. So easy. So good!

Makes 6 to 8 servings

Spring Cake

1 stick margarine
½ cup vegetable oil
¼ cup unsweetened cocoa powder
1 cup water
1 teaspoon cinnamon
2 cups all-purpose flour

2 cups sugar
½ cup buttermilk with 1 teaspoon baking soda added
2 eggs
1 teaspoon vanilla
½ teaspoon salt

In a large saucepan bring the first 4 ingredients to a boil. Remove from stove and add the remaining ingredients, mixing well. Pour into a greased and floured 13 × 9-inch baking pan and bake at 400° F 20 to 25 minutes.

Frosting

1 stick margarine

⅓ cup buttermilk

¼ cup unsweetened cocoa powder

1 box powdered sugar

1 teaspoon vanilla

Nuts, if desired

Bring to a boil in a saucepan the margarine, buttermilk, and cocoa. Beat in the powdered sugar and vanilla and pour on cake while still warm. Top with nuts, if desired. At our house we bake this cake on the day that a family member sees the first sign of spring.

Makes 24 servings

INDEX

Video Tape Available

The Once-a-Month Cooking method is available on video tape for small group or individual use. For information write: Once-a-Month Cooking Video, 7153 West Walden Drive, Littleton, CO 80123, or phone (303) 979-8132.